A Passport to Cheese is your personal culinary adventure, sure to delight your taste buds and celebrate everyone's favorite ingredient—no planes, trains, or automobiles required. In his second cookbook, Afrim Pristine, bestselling author and owner of Toronto's beloved Cheese Boutique, has gathered global flavors and international cheese-making traditions in 75 delicious recipes. Here he highlights everything from creamy French camembert, fresh Mexican queso fresco, and soft Italian ricotta, to sharp English cheddar, salty Cypriot halloumi, and robust Canadian Celtic Blue.

- **Cheese all day:** Whether you're looking for breakfast, lunch, appetizers, dinner, dessert, or even cocktail pairings, you'll find the perfect cheese-focused recipe.
- **75 internationally inspired recipes:** Try a French croque monsieur with nutty Comté for an indulgent lunch, a Jamaican jerk spice macaroni pie with 5-year aged cheddar for dinner, and a Spanish Basque cheesecake for dessert.
- **Shop with confidence:** With a comprehensive glossary featuring photos of all the cheeses referenced in the book (and a special list of Afrim's top 13 favorites), along with storage information and helpful facts about flavor profiles and countries of origin, you'll know which cheese to buy and how to keep it fresh.
- **Build the cheese board of your dreams!** Afrim has included a full chapter of 10 differently themed boards showcasing cheeses from various countries, as well as guidance on how to develop and build a cheese board of your own.

With Afrim as your tour guide, you're guaranteed an unforgettable journey as you discover the world of cheese. You'll love his inexhaustible passion that leaps off the page, the incredible recipes suitable for every skill level, and the gorgeous photography that is sure to transport you across the globe. Come along for the ride with this must-have cookbook, an essential addition to your own cheese-loving library, and the perfect gift for every cheese lover in your life.

CHEESE SPOTLIGHT: PIAVE (p. 24)

A PASSPORT TO CHEESE

75 INSPIRING RECIPES FROM AROUND THE WORLD

AFRIM PRISTINE

appetite
by RANDOM HOUSE

Library and Archives Canada Cataloguing in Publication is available upon request.

ISBN: 9780525612407
eBook ISBN: 9780525612414

Photography by Paula Wilson
Book and cover design by Talia Abramson
Typeset by Erin Cooper
Food styling by Heather Shaw
Prop styling by Oksana Slavutych

Printed in China

The authorized representative in the EU for product safety and compliance is Penguin Random House Ireland, Morrison Chambers, 32 Nassau Street, Dublin D02 YH68, Ireland, https://eu-contact.penguin.ie

Published in Canada by Appetite by Random House®,
a division of Penguin Random House Canada Limited.
320 Front Street West, Suite 1400
Toronto, Ontario, M5V 3B6, Canada
penguinrandomhouse.ca

10 9 8 7 6 5 4 3 2 1

appetite
by RANDOM HOUSE

Penguin
Random House
Canada

To all the cheese lovers out there, and the cheese makers
I've worked with over the years. Also, to the whole Pristine
and Cheese Boutique family; my supportive wife, Courtney;
and my sweet boy, Leonardo: I love you with all my heart.
This one is for you.

CHEESE SPOTLIGHT: PECORINO ROMANO & PARMIGIANO REGGIANO (see pp. 23–24)

CONTENTS

ARGENTINA
TURKEY
ANKARA INTERNATIONAL AIRPORT
WELCOME
USA
ARRIVAL
GREECE
ATHENS
CANADA
BIENVENUE AU
DENMARK
COPENHAGEN
SOUTH KOREA
ARRIVAL
YPRUS
WELCOME TO NEW DELHI
INDIA
CONTROL
PORTUG
LISBON
SPAIN
ARRIVAL

Afrim Pristine
CHEESE BOUTIQUE
IGOR
Gorgonzola
DOLCE
Donna
ASIAGO

INTRODUCTION

Every cheese tells a story.

Every cheese tells a story—of the place it's made, of the people who make it, and, of course, of the people who eat it. I've loved these stories for my whole life, and they've taken me around the world and back home again. You could also say that they are stories I was born to tell.

By the time my parents had me and my three brothers, the family business was up and running. Cheese Boutique was born out of the experience my father and grandfather had running a convenience store in Toronto's West End. They realized there was a hunger (pun intended) in the city for more international products, particularly cheese. I got to see how much my dad respected the cheese makers he bought from, and how that appreciation translated to our customers. I grew up in and around Cheese Boutique stores, first on Bloor Street, then a little farther west, then eventually to our current spaces on Ripley Avenue. I learned about cheese and the business of selling it alongside my dad and my brother Agim.

But putting cheese aside for a quick second, it was my mother who first got me excited about cooking. She was born in Avellino, Italy, just outside Naples. My brothers and I pretty much grew up Neopolitan. We didn't have ketchup or mustard in the house, ever; we had my mother's homemade sun-dried tomato pesto or her famous San Marzano tomato sauce. I would always watch and help my mom in the kitchen. I know every chef says something like that, but for real, this was my childhood. As she cooked, she seemed to float through the kitchen. She made rustic, and sometimes complex, dishes but she did it with ease. Even today, she can out-cook anyone I know. And as I grew up and entered my twenties and then my thirties, my education deepened after spending time in Europe and across North America.

I trained at some of the best cheese factories and producers on the planet, learning from the best cheese makers and affineurs (people who age cheese). And by the time I was thirty-two, I was the world's youngest *maître fromager*, as it's called in French, or cheese master in English. Still, to this day, I travel to discover new cheeses, to see and meet with old colleagues, and to learn about what different cultures and regions are doing with cheese.

But back then, I brought that experience back home and poured it into our family business. Receiving this maître fromager title was a huge deal not only for me and Cheese Boutique, but for the cheese industry in Canada. It is a worldwide recognition that everyone in the cheese industry aims to achieve. The French just don't hand it out to anyone and everyone, and I felt blessed to have received it. It also added fuel to my fire—I needed to do more, I needed to keep waving the cheese flag all around the world, and I needed to keep growing and honing my craft.

While traveling for work, I would always try and sneak into kitchens, whether it was at a dairy or a local restaurant in town. I would do random stages (like an internship) at restaurants, as I never went to cooking school because of my hectic schedule at the family business, and this work gave me the real-life cooking experience I was craving. I got to cook with and learn from chefs like Daniel Boulud, Mark McEwan, Lynn Crawford, and Alain Ducasse—just to name a few! I did any job I was told to do by my superiors. But it was when the chefs would start grating cheese, melting cheese, or manipulating cheese that I got the most excited. Because, working at Cheese Boutique, I had to learn as much as I could about the ingredients we sold. We sell 10,000 different products from all over the world, and I made it my job to know what they taste like and what they pair with. Add this knowledge to learning different culinary techniques from my mentors, along with traveling and discovering cuisines from all over the world, and it seems only natural that a book like this—one that centers cheese as the star ingredient and explores its importance on a global scale—was in my future.

I've never stopped wanting to know more about cheese and how it relates to culture and cuisine, and I don't think I'll ever stop learning. Because when you think of how simple cheese is—milk and salt, that's it—it's crazy to think of how many different kinds there are. Although cheese is simple in theory, the myriad details that come into play in its creation make it complex and fascinating. At least to me! I call this "cheese magic."

I've never stopped wanting to know more about cheese and how it relates to culture and cuisine, and I don't think I'll ever stop learning.

Every cheese starts with a place: the mountains of Switzerland, the pastures of England, the rocky terrain of Greece. You may have heard the term "terroir" used in reference to wine. That same concept applies to cheese. Everything in the environment—from the climate, to the soil and landscape, to the plants that grow there—will have an impact on the cheese. And the very first impact is the kind of animals that can be raised on the land. Cows need a lot of space and, for as much of the year as possible, grass to graze. Sheep and goats, on the other hand, can be farmed on smaller parcels of land and require far fewer calories per day compared to cows. So right away you can see how the geography of an area will dictate what kind of animals—and therefore milk—each region will be starting out with.

And from that starting place of terroir and animals comes a cheese that suits the people of the region. If you're raising goats and sheep in the hot climate of Greece, it makes sense to create fresh and young cheeses like feta or halloumi that are a perfect accent to the other produce being grown there, like olives, tomatoes, and lemons. On the other end of the terroir scale, imagine Switzerland. You have access to alpine meadows for your cows to graze in the summer. You can take that milk and make gruyère, which will take months if not years to mature and is perfect for melting into fondue or raclette.

But, like with the chicken or the egg, I often ask myself, what came first? In the first example, was it the idea of what we now call a Greek salad, or was it the actual cheese, feta? Did feta inspire the salad, or did the terroir and climate inspire the salad? Conversely, Swiss cheeses are great for melting, so was fondue created because the cheeses in Switzerland are conducive to this dish, or was it because the climate and terroir in Switzerland scream for some warm, melty cheese and a baguette dipped into it? What a cheesy conundrum, am I right?

The culture and cuisine of a region will also affect how people consume cheese. French cuisine is known for technique and refinement, and so are its cheeses. There are hundreds of French cheeses, and every region has varieties it's been making for hundreds of years. Cheese is eaten in sandwiches and in recipes, of course, but mostly it is considered special enough to be enjoyed on its own. It's frequently served after dinner in lieu of dessert. What better way to finish off that beautiful red wine you had with dinner?

Indian cuisine is all about spices. Every area, even every household, has its own blend of spices that have been passed down from generation to generation. The dishes call for a simple, fresh cheese that can take and soak up those rich, bold flavors. And so you wind up with paneer, a fresh curd cheese that adds heft to many vegetarian dishes.

When you think about the marriage of cheese and culture, you can understand why certain preferences—even rules—develop. Many Italians believe that eating cheese with fish or seafood is just wrong. Okay, but what about lox and cream cheese on a bagel? Don't tell me that's not one of the best combinations of all time. I have chef friends in Japan, Vietnam, and South Korea who tell me it's hard to find a good cheese board in these countries unless you've got access to a high-end French restaurant. However, they also report that, more and more, cheese is showing up as an integral ingredient in a recipe. And it makes sense—people travel and migrate now more than ever before. With those movements around the world, people learn about new culinary cultures and bring their own along. For example, an influx of Norwegians to Wisconsin over 100 years ago

resulted in an American love for Jarlsberg. I recently visited a Thai restaurant run by a young chef who moved from Thailand to British Columbia and combined her two cultures by adding mozzarella to pad thai, and I loved it.

I've spent my life learning about cheese; how it's made, all the foundational elements that bring it together, and the cuisines it fits into. And I have nothing but respect for the traditions of cheese making. But I'm also thrilled when I discover a new way to think about cheese and how best to enjoy it. I hope this book gives you a chance to learn the stories of cheese from around the world and how you can tell those stories in your home with your family. I feel truly thankful to each and every one of you for taking this cheese journey with me.

Afrim Pristine

THE FAMOUS CLIMATIZED CHEESE-AGING VAULT AT CHEESE BOUTIQUE

Camembert
Mon Père
EPOISSES
BERTHAUT
BRESSE
BLEU
Chaumes Le Crémier
$10.99/ea
Bresse Bleu
$5.99/ea
Pont – L'eveque
$18.99/ea
Caprice des Dieux
$6.99/ea
CHAUMES
BERTHAUT
SOUMAINTRAIN
Chaource
Lincet
PONT-L'ÉVÊQUE
E. GRAINDORGE
Brillat-Savarin
$25.99/ea
LIVAROT AOP
E. GRAINDORGE
Saint-André
$7.99/ea
L'AMI DU CHAMBERTIN
LANGRES
AOP
Carré du Berry
Excellence

A CHEESY ATLAS

Pack your bags! Here comes my non-exhaustive list of key cheese-making regions of the world. The recipes you'll find in this book use cheeses from the countries discussed below, but I hope you'll think of this list as a starting point to fuel your own cheese explorations. There is so much to discover.

ARGENTINA

Beef is king in Argentina, and the country's cuisine is known for grilling. The same goes for its cheese. Provola, an offshoot of Italy's provolone, is a mild, firm cheese. It takes on flavors beautifully, which is why it's so great to grill—it can take on the taste of the smoke it's cooked over and the salsa verdes or chimichurris it's served with. It's an excellent vegetarian alternative to steak, but in Argentina it's often served as an appetizer before the meat comes out. Provola is not a cheese to be eaten on its own, the way cheddar or brie are enjoyed, but as a backdrop to big flavors.

CANADA

Most Canadian cheeses come from Ontario and Quebec, in central Canada. But just like the cultures and languages of our two largest provinces, their cheeses have differences. With its English heritage, Ontario is known for cheddar. And, if I may say, Ontario cheddar is some of the best in the world. More recently, there's been an increase in Dutch-style and Swiss-style cheese making in Ontario. Again, those northern European varieties just make sense in the cold Ontario climate. Quebec, with obvious connection to France, makes a wider variety of cheeses. Although cheese curds, with their after-the-bar poutine associations, may be the most well-known Quebec cheese, the province's cheese makers excel at all the refined styles found in France.

Elsewhere in the country, Prince Edward Island and British Columbia have really been making cheesy moves over the last 25 years or so. On both coasts, small-batch, artisanal cheeses are coming to the forefront. They may not be the Canadian cheese superpowers of Ontario and Quebec, but they sure are making tasty products.

CYPRUS

This small island off the coast of Turkey is known for halloumi, which is made with a combination of goat's and sheep's milk. Once hard to find in North America, this firm, salty cheese has recently taken off. Expect it to be as ubiquitous as burrata on restaurant menus one day soon. This cheese is most often grilled, but can also be eaten straight up. It takes on the flavors of the smoke it's cooked over, or it can be perfectly pan-seared with olive oil, citrus, and fresh herbs. Like Argentina's provola cheese, it's an excellent swap for steak for a vegetarian barbecue dish.

DENMARK

Two cheeses define Denmark, and they couldn't be more different. Danish Blue is known around the world. It's not too strong or stinky, and it melts and blends into other foods easily. The other is havarti, loved for its mild flavor, irregular holes, and semisoft texture. Like Dutch cheeses, havarti is often infused with other flavors like dill or peppers. Danish people eat cheese all day, either as a snack or as part of the open-faced sandwiches (smørrebrød) Denmark is known for. For a small country, both in population and in geographic size, Denmark is mighty in cheese production, exporting both of these cheese superstars worldwide.

ENGLAND

Among England's gifts to the world—the steam engine, Shakespeare, the Beatles (though I'm a Rolling Stones guy myself)—cheddar must surely top the list. Originating in the village of Cheddar in the 12th century, it eventually traveled the globe and became the world's most popular cheese. Although the English make over 750 different varieties of cheese, they are known for hard cheeses like cheddar, Red Leicester, and Lancashire. These cheeses are pressed to remove moisture, which means they keep very well. A notable exception is stilton, a creamy yet crumbly, powerful blue cheese. Like the French, the English enjoy their cheeses without a lot of fuss or other components. Whether it's on a cart that's wheeled around a fine-dining restaurant after dinner or in a ploughman's lunch at the pub, the English are happy to eat their cheese with just a glass of port or a pint of beer, or as part of a larger meal.

FRANCE

It's difficult to think of a country where cheese is more integrated into daily life than France. The average French person consumes close to 60 pounds of cheese per year! Which is easier to understand when you consider that it's frequently consumed at every meal and is often its own course.

Cheese making—and eating—is so much a part of their cultural DNA that the French excel at every style. Each region has a particular climate, terroir (meaning the environment of that area), and livestock population, which means the range of cheeses made across the country is vast. Some 400 varieties are made in France, from the creamy camemberts of Normandy, to the sharp and nutty Comté made in the mountains near the Swiss border, to the delicate goat cheeses of the Loire Valley.

Like French cuisine, French cheeses are highly technical to make and are often very refined in their presentation. Here you'll find some of the most beautiful-looking cheeses, from the cheese itself to the packaging, and they're meant to be appreciated on their own. Yes, you can cook with French cheeses, but a great many of them are intended to be savored with only a glass of wine—another thing the French are pretty good at making.

GREECE

The cheeses made in Greece are a perfect complement to the country: a small, mountainous landscape on the Mediterranean. Oh, and it's hot. What do you feel like eating in a warm climate? How about salad? Fresh, young cheeses are fantastic with tomatoes, cucumbers, lemons, olives, and olive oil (other great products of Greece). Now, how about livestock? You can't raise cattle without lots of space and pastures, but sheep and goats do just fine on rocky terrain. Add it all together and it's only logical that you end up with cheeses like feta and myzithra—they belong in Greece! Feta's importance in Greece is protected by the European Union's PDO (protected designation of origin), meaning any similar cheese made in Canada or in the US can only ever be feta-style, not traditional feta. Unlike French cheeses, which can be enjoyed on their own or with a glass of wine, Greek cheeses are meant to be enjoyed as part of a meal.

INDIA

A few cheeses come from India, but paneer is by far the most popular and well known. Made from curdled milk, paneer has a texture something like Cyprus's halloumi or Canada's cheese curds: it squeaks when you bite into it. This mild and non-melting cheese is an excellent companion for the aromatic spices of Indian cuisine. It keeps its shape in curries and in dishes like saag paneer, a rich spinach dish.

ITALY

When thinking of Italian cheeses, it's all about depth, not breadth. Italy makes nowhere near the range of varieties that France does, but on the other hand, the country makes some of the world's most important cheeses: Parmigiano-Reggiano, pecorino romano, and Grana Padano. Northern Italians created that style of hard, salty cheeses meant to be finely grated over pasta. The cheeses of the south—mozzarella, ricotta, burrata—are soft and mild and perfect for melting on pizza or starring in a salad.

Perhaps more than any other country, Italians use cheese in their pastries and desserts. Think cannoli or tiramisu made from ricotta and mascarpone. And it's because of the worldwide popularity of Italian food that these cheeses have become household staples. Italians' love of cheese is ancient. During the Roman Empire, some wealthy households had a *caseale*—a kitchen dedicated to cheese making!

Fun fact: Gorgonzola and ricotta date back 2,000 years, with cheese-making techniques refined during the Roman Empire. Also, like feta in Greece, Italy's iconic cheeses like Parmigiano-Reggiano and pecorino romano are controlled by PDO (protected designation of origin) status, ensuring authenticity and traditional production methods. This means, if it ain't broke, don't fix it.

JAMAICA

Jamaica is not a cheese-making country, but cheese is still central to the culture and cuisine. When I think of Jamaican food, I think of macaroni pie: a rich, zesty, baked version of mac and cheese. It's a classic at family gatherings and makes a perfect side dish for spicy mains like jerk chicken.

MEXICO

The cuisine of Mexico is highly cheese-centric, whether we're talking about Michelin-starred fine dining or the delicious street food we're all addicted to. Their cheeses—cotija, Oaxaca, and queso fresco, to name a few—are usually integrated into dishes and rarely eaten on their own. Crumbly, salty cotija is grated over grilled corn; stringy, melty Oaxaca cheese melts perfectly in a tamale; soft, fresh queso fresco is sprinkled over salads or guacamole. The list goes on!

THE NETHERLANDS

The Netherlands makes some of the most recognizable and popular cheeses in the world: gouda, beemster, and edam. They don't make endless varieties of cheese, but they are masters of these three cheeses, while also being masters of infusions. They flavor their cheeses with pesto, truffle, mustard, asparagus, nettles, or even odd flavors like bacon, wasabi, and so many more ingredients. At Cheese Boutique, we have at least twenty-five different infused cheeses from the Netherlands! Cheese is enjoyed simply in the Netherlands: on bread with jam for breakfast. I will also add that a few slices of smoked gouda on a smashed burger is wickedly good.

PORTUGAL

The Portuguese are incredibly proud of their cheeses. Every little nook and cranny of that country makes cheese, and the products vary wildly from region to region. If you've never tried Portuguese cheese it's because most of this country's cheese is consumed there, with only a small portion being exported. Most mainland cheeses are made with goat's or sheep's milk, and cheeses made on the Atlantic archipelago of the Azores are made from cow's milk. The most well-known Portuguese cheese is São Jorge, which is made with milk from cows that graze on grass 365 days a year. It's a firm cheese that tastes like grass and ocean, which makes sense since it's made in the Azores. Soft and buttery Serra da Estrela sheep's milk cheese is made in the mountains of the same name. Serpa is a firm, pecorino-like sheep's milk cheese made in the southern region of Alentejo.

SOUTH KOREA

The cuisine in South Korea is so unique. With obvious South Asian influences and the use of classic ingredients like kimchi, sesame oil, and gochujang, South Korean dishes didn't start involving cheese until the Korean war in the 1950s. During that time, American soldiers started giving cheese to the population as a quick and cheap source of protein. Naturally, this led to the fusion of cheese into classics like bibimbap, rice dishes, and the now-famous cheese dakgalbi. A few small producers now even receive "K-cheese certification" for the products being made in Korea, all in cheese science laboratories.

SPAIN

Manchego. If someone asks you to name a Spanish cheese, that's your choice, right? Cheese making in Spain complements the cuisine of this mostly hot country with a love of late-night, grazing-style dinners. The Spanish, famously, eat late. Like, really late. You meet your friends at a bar, stand up at a tall table, and order tapas. Grilled octopus, a few slices of jamón (cured pork), a small bowl of olives, and a chunk of cheese, along with a glass of beer or wine. Rich and crumbly manchego is made in the region of La Mancha using only milk from Manchega sheep. With Spanish influence around the world, manchego might arguably be one of the top 5 most recognizable cheeses worldwide. It's everywhere.

That said, to discover the real cheese gems of Spain, you need to travel there, especially to some of the smaller towns. Mahón, Garrotxa, and Majorero cheeses are amazing but very difficult to find outside Spain. Two famous blue cheeses are also made in Spain: Valdeón and Cabrales. They are both huge, fiery blue cheeses that are not for the faint of heart. These cheeses can clear your sinuses instantly. I guess the Spanish just keep the good stuff to themselves. I can respect that.

SWITZERLAND

What comes to mind when you think of this small, land-locked country, smack in the middle of Europe? Mountains, chocolates, watches, banking, and, oh yeah, cheese. It wouldn't insult the Swiss to say that they're not the most inventive culture. Rather, they do what they've been doing forever, making what suits the culture and the climate, and they do it very, very well.

Cheese is a regional pursuit in Switzerland, with cantons (the regions that make up the country) each making their own specialty. Emmental, what most people recognize as Swiss cheese with its iconic holes (also known as eyes), comes from Bern. Creamy, nutty gruyère, made from a combination of milk collected in the morning and the evening, comes from Fribourg. Eponymous Appenzeller gets its assertive flavor from the brine rubbed onto the exterior of the wheel.

Most cheeses from Switzerland are great melters and perfect for that very Swiss dish called fondue. Of all the countries I've ever traveled to, Switzerland takes its cheese more seriously than any other.

THAILAND

You might not think of cheese when you think of Thai food. Honestly, I didn't either until I had an incredible meal at Baan Lao in Richmond, British Columbia. Chef Nutcha Phanthoupheng made traditional pad thai and topped it with a layer of grated fresh mozzarella. My mind was blown! I've since learned that cheese is being used more often in Thailand in dishes like cheese hot pots and omelets, and is making its way to Thai restaurants around the world.

TURKEY

Turkey's cuisine reflects its position as the cultural (and literal) crossroads of Europe, Asia, the Middle East, and the Balkans. As do its cheeses. Most Turkish cheese is eaten within a recipe or alongside many other foods in a meal. At breakfast, they eat *beyaz peynir*, translated as "white cheese," along with cucumbers, tomatoes, olives, and simit (Turkey's version of a bagel). Beyaz peynir is also baked into savory pastries called börek. For dessert, they use a soft, stringy cheese called hatay to make what I can only describe as a cheese-filled baklava and to make künefe, a warm, sweet treat.

UNITED STATES

American cheese is a high/low story. The country is the biggest producer of cheese in the world, making a whopping 6.5 metric tons annually. A huge portion of that production is what I'd call industrial cheese. It's the mozzarella on your pizza, the cheddar in your burrito, and the bright orange slice on your burger. It's not fancy, but it serves as a delicious means to an end.

On the other hand, you'll also find world-class cheeses made in the US. It's a vast country with a wide range of climates and cultures. That being said, the cheese-making areas are quite limited: California, Oregon, Vermont, and, of course, Wisconsin. They don't wear those cheese hats at the Green Bay Packers' games for nothing. Wisconsin is the cheese capital of America, using up nearly 90 percent of the state's milk supply to create 2 billion pounds of cheese annually. The state is known for cheddar, Colby, brick cheese, and cheese curds, among others. These cheeses make sense for the climate and cuisine of this northern state, but they're also enjoyed across the country. Farther east, Vermont makes a similar range of cheeses. And in the west, California, with its hot climate and produce-forward cuisine, excels in goat cheese, while Oregon has become known for its award-winning blue cheese.

CHEESE 101

BUYING, STORING & SERVING

Well, you've planned out your first cheese-sourcing trip (even if you aren't leaving your home city). Before you get on that plane, train, or automobile, there are a few details to think through. Allow me to guide you.

HOW TO BUY CHEESE

You might think that a guy who sells cheese would encourage unbridled cheese shopping. But you'd be wrong! Once a piece of cheese is cut from the wheel, it's not going to improve. In fact, the opposite is likely true. If it's not eaten soon after you purchase it, the cheese will dry out. So, first of all, find a proper cheese shop that will help you practice restraint. Get the level of service you deserve!

Once you've found a great place, visit frequently rather than stockpiling. I know it's exciting to see all those options, but you want to choose quality over quantity. For example, try buying 5 oz (140 g) of three different cheeses. Next time, try three more. And so on. And how do you choose those cheeses? Get to know your cheesemonger. Find out what they like and share your own preferences. That will allow them to guide you through the wide world of cheese. Tell them what you're planning to use the cheese for. Is it to add to a salad? Grate on top of pasta? Pair with a certain wine? The more information you give, the better advice you'll receive. Trust them like you'd trust your doctor!

HOW TO STORE CHEESE

For all you real cheese fanatics, buying a vacuum sealer for a few hundred dollars will save you from cheese that's gone past its prime. That's the most ideal way to store cheese and keep it fresh at optimal quality. You can also find fancy cheese storage bags online or at cheese shops. The texture of the bag prevents oxidization and helps keep the cheese fresh.

Both of the above options are wonderful, but they cost money and will continue to do so, as you'll need to buy vacuum sealer bags and cheese storage bags. If you want to use low-cost items you've already got around the house, turn to parchment paper and aluminum foil. You can also keep the cheese in the packaging you

MY FAVORITE KNIVES

1 Serrated baguette knife. Nothing goes better with cheese than crusty bread!

2 Cheese fork. This is to grab harder cheeses off of a cheese board

3 Bloomy rind cheese knife. This is for cutting cheeses like Délice de Bourgogne, Chaource, or camembert.

4 Medium-sized blade. This is part of a set (see knife 12), used to cut beemster or gouda.

5 Prosciutto and serrano ham knife.

6 Pecorino knife.

7 Small-format, delicate cheese knife. This works well with goat cheese.

8 Large-format, softer cheese knife. This works for larger wheels of brie or triple crème.

9 My personalized maître fromager chisel, for large-format hard cheeses.

10 Cheese pick, for a cheese board

11 Bougie butter knife.

12 Medium-sized blade, used to cut semi-firm wheels.

bought it in—often cheese wax paper. This will hold moisture in the cheese for a few days. After that, you should rewrap your cheese in parchment paper and then aluminum foil. This will allow it to breathe but won't let the aromas from the other food in your fridge permeate the cheese. Try to avoid plastic wrap. It's fine for the first few days, but after that your cheese will taste like your fridge and the other items in your fridge will taste like your cheese. Plastic also doesn't prevent the cheese from drying out and oxidizing.

HOW TO SERVE CHEESE

Eating cheese straight from the fridge is not a good idea. Having your cheese out for at least 2 hours first is best, as this allows it to really open up to its true, full form. I've trained with cheese makers who barely refrigerate their cheeses at all—so hardcore! I'm not asking you to do that, but know that the longer you can let your cheese sit, the better. Think of it like wine. When you've spent your hard-earned money on a good bottle of red, you want to decant it for 2 or 3 hours so the true flavors shine. Bringing cheese to room temperature is showing it the respect you'd show that wine. And to really show your cheese respect, check out the Cheese Boards chapter (pp. 170–195) for more information.

Cheese Tools & Knives

As a cheesemonger, I've learned to use every cheese knife in different capacities. There are certain knives or tools for different styles of cheese. Whether you are a cheese novice, cheese professional, someone who loves to break down larger wheels, or just someone who loves making cheese boards at home for entertaining, all these tools will be of use to you. When cheese is cut properly with the right tools, it's not a matter of strength, it's a matter of knowing how to use each knife. I'm obviously not a surgeon, but I imagine that a surgeon does the same with their tools when performing different cuts and incisions.

If you have been to a high-end or Michelin-starred restaurant that has a cheese trolley, you might recognize some of these knives and tools. In fact, the places that do proper French-style cheese service are so exacting that the fromager will use a different knife to portion each cheese.

Over the years, I've accumulated probably twenty-five cheese knives—some of them made for me specifically, and others given to me by mentors. My fave is my "AP" chisel, received in 2013 when I was awarded the title of maître fromager. The truth is, you can go to a high-end boutique that sells all kinds of specialized cheese knife sets, or you can go online and get a beginner set that will get you started. IKEA has some nice stuff too. If you make cheese boards, it's nice to have a designated set of knives to serve your guests and show them you've made an effort with both the ingredients and presentation.

1
2
3
4
5
6
7
8
9
10
11
12

CHEESE GLOSSARY

On the following pages, you'll find a breakdown of some of my favorite cheeses. Use this to help you shop or discover something new. As you read on, I'm sure you'll have a moment when you realize that a cheese you love isn't included. People feel a real sense of loyalty to the cheeses they love, and I'm no different. But with thousands of cheeses in the world, I've built the recipes in this book to hopefully capture some of my and your favorites and to expose you to new sources of inspiration. It's impossible to describe them fully in just a few words, so feel free to mark up these pages with your own notes.

5 BROTHERS (CANADA)
MILK: Cow, pasteurized
FLAVOR: Nutty, smooth, medium-bodied
RECIPE: Ontario Cheese Board (p. 189)
FUN FACT: You can take a fantastic tour of Gunn's Hill Artisan Cheese, the producer of this cheese.

ASIAGO (ITALY)
MILK: Cow, pasteurized
FLAVOR: Sharp, rich, medium-bodied
RECIPE: The Mighty Negroni with Italian Asiago (p. 157)
FUN FACT: The pride of northern Italy and one of the oldest Italian cheese recipes.

BEAUFORT (FRANCE)
MILK: Cow, unpasteurized
FLAVOR: Smooth, mild, buttery
RECIPE: Parisian Green Bay Packers Soup (p. 59)
FUN FACT: Like many Alpine cheeses, Beaufort is made in large wheels, weighing as much as 130 pounds!

BEEMSTER (THE NETHERLANDS)
MILK: Cow, pasteurized FLAVOR: Sharp, nutty, bold
RECIPES: Good Morning Dutch Quiche (p. 43), Beemster & Onion Tarts (p. 79), Kaaskroketten or Dutch-Style Crispy Croquettes (p. 83), Dutch Mule with 2-Year Aged Beemster (p. 162), All-Dutch Cheese Board (p. 194)
FUN FACT: The older the beemster, the more complex the flavor.

BEL HAVEN TRIPLE CRÈME BRIE (CANADA)
MILK: Cow, pasteurized
FLAVOR: Mild, buttery, creamy
RECIPE: Ontario Cheese Board (p. 189)
FUN FACT: This has become one of Ontario's best triple cream cheeses.

BLEU D'AUVERGNE (FRANCE)
MILK: Cow, unpasteurized
FLAVOR: Creamy, bold, robust
RECIPE: Stollen & Blue Cheese Holiday Dessert (p. 141)
FUN FACT: A cousin to Roquefort, this blue cheese is made in the famous Rhône Valley wine region.

BOCCONCINI OR FRESH MOZZARELLA (ITALY)
MILK: Cow, pasteurized
FLAVOR: Mild, fresh, delicate
RECIPE: A Canadian Cheesy Caesar (p. 166)
FUN FACT: Like burrata and bufala mozzarella, bocconcini is best at its freshest.

BRIE DE MEAUX (FRANCE)
MILK: Cow, unpasteurized
FLAVOR: Funky, creamy, ripe
RECIPE: All-French Cheese Board (p. 177)
FUN FACT: This was the first, and is still the most traditional, recipe for brie.

BRILLO (ITALY)
MILK: Sheep, pasteurized
FLAVOR: Floral, salty, medium-bodied
RECIPE: The Ultimate Italian Cheese Board (p. 193)
FUN FACT: This cheese is soaked and aged in Chianti from Tuscany.

BUFALA MOZZARELLA (ITALY)
MILK: Water buffalo, pasteurized
FLAVOR: Fresh, milky, delicate
RECIPES: Bufala & Peaches (p. 56), My Turkish Family Künefe (p. 146)
FUN FACT: Find out when your cheesemonger gets their fresh mozzarella shipment, then enjoy this cheese 5–7 days after that.

BURRATA (ITALY)
MILK: Cow, pasteurized
FLAVOR: Fresh, delicate, milky
RECIPES: Nick's Burrata & Peas (p. 87), Bougie Burrata (p. 84)
FUN FACT: Always drain your burrata for 1 hour before using it.

CAMEMBERT (FRANCE)
MILK: Cow, unpasteurized
FLAVOR: Mushroomy, earthy, aromatic
RECIPE: Normandy Baked Camembert (p. 48)
FUN FACT: Look for the AOC or AOP government designation to be sure you're getting traditional cheese from Normandy.

CELTIC BLUE (CANADA)
MILK: Cow, pasteurized
FLAVOR: Sharp, full-bodied, salty
RECIPE: Ontario Cheese Board (p. 189)
FUN FACT: This cheese was inspired by stilton made in England.

CHABICHOU (FRANCE)
MILK: Goat, unpasteurized
FLAVOR: Funky, aromatic, perfectly sour and salty
RECIPE: All-French Cheese Board (p. 177)
FUN FACT: This is a pioneer of the goat cheese world.

CHEDDAR (ENGLAND)
MILK: Cow, pasteurized
FLAVOR: Funky, sharp
RECIPES: English-Style Potted Cheese (p. 60), After-Dinner English Cheese Board (p. 190)
FUN FACT: The town of Somerset is the birthplace of cheddar.

CHEDDAR (UNITED STATES)
MILK: Cow, pasteurized
FLAVOR: Sharp, salty, aged
RECIPE: Parisian Green Bay Packers Soup (p. 59)
FUN FACT: The state of Wisconsin produces more cheese than many whole countries.

CHEESE CURDS (CANADA)

MILK: Cow, pasteurized

FLAVOR: Squeaky, mild, tangy

RECIPE: Duck Confit Poutine (p. 127)

FUN FACT: Refrigerated curds lose their texture, so buy curds as fresh as you can and use them right away.

COMTÉ (FRANCE)

MILK: Cow, unpasteurized **FLAVOR:** Buttery, sharp, nutty

RECIPES: Croque Monsieur (p. 72), French 75 with Comté (p. 158), All-French Cheese Board (p. 177), Prosciutto Lovers with a Side of Cheese (p. 185)

FUN FACT: Comté is the only cheese to be aged in le Fort des Rousses, one of the largest aging caves on the planet.

CREAM CHEESE (CANADA)

MILK: Cow, pasteurized

FLAVOR: Mild, fresh, creamy

RECIPES: Open-Faced French Omelet (p. 35), Maple, Bacon & Blue Cheese Cheeseball (p. 80), Basque Cheesecake (p. 149)

FUN FACT: The higher the milk fat, the better the cream cheese.

ERMITE BLUE (CANADA)

MILK: Cow, pasteurized

FLAVOR: Salty, mild, light-bodied for a blue cheese

RECIPE: Quebec Cheese Board (p. 181)

FUN FACT: This is one of the cheeses that sparked the Canadian cheese boom in the early 2000s.

FETA (GREECE)

MILK: Half sheep, half goat, pasteurized

FLAVOR: Salty, perfectly sweet, well balanced

RECIPES: Greek Scrambled Eggs (p. 36), Late-for-Work Green Eggs (p. 39), Greek Bruschetta a.k.a. Dakos (p. 51), Marinated Mediterranean Feta (p. 67)

FUN FACT: Feta-style cheeses are made in many countries, including Turkey, Albania, Italy, Montenegro, and even France, but Greek feta is a protected name, like champagne.

FRIULANO (ITALY)
MILK: Cow, pasteurized
FLAVOR: Mild, delicate, easy to eat
RECIPE: Spritz O'Clock & Snacks (p. 182)
FUN FACT: A traditional northern Italian cheese, made in the region of Friuli.

GOAT CHEESE (CANADA & UNITED STATES)
MILK: Goat, pasteurized
FLAVOR: Fresh, fluffy, sour
RECIPE: Poached Rhubarb & Goat Cheese (p. 137)
FUN FACT: Goat's milk is low in lactose, making it one of the easiest to digest, even for those with a lactose sensitivity.

GORGONZOLA (ITALY)
MILK: Cow, pasteurized
FLAVOR: Sharp, salty, creamy
RECIPE: The Ultimate Italian Cheese Board (p. 193)
FUN FACT: This spicy blue cheese is one of the oldest cheese recipes in Italy.

GOUDA (THE NETHERLANDS)
MILK: Cow, pasteurized
FLAVOR: Mild, sweet, medium-bodied
RECIPES: Good Morning Dutch Quiche (p. 43), 5-Cheese Mac & Cheese (p. 108), All-Dutch Cheese Board (p. 194)
FUN FACT: All gouda made in the Netherlands is naturally lactose-free.

GREY OWL (CANADA)
MILK: Goat, pasteurized
FLAVOR: Fresh, creamy, lush
RECIPE: Quebec Cheese Board (p. 181)
FUN FACT: When people learned that this was Meghan Markle's favorite cheese, it became the best-selling goat cheese in Canada.

GRUYÈRE (SWITZERLAND)
MILK: Cow, unpasteurized
FLAVOR: Nutty, fruity, sharp
RECIPES: Bougie Euro-Style Grilled Cheese (p. 75), 5-Cheese Mac & Cheese (p. 108), Romantic Date Night Fondue for Two (p. 111)
FUN FACT: AOP-controlled, gruyère is made only in Switzerland and France.

HALLOUMI (CYPRUS)

MILK: Sheep and cow blend, pasteurized

FLAVOR: Salty, tangy, medium-bodied

RECIPES: Afrim & Courtney's Thai Halloumi Rice (p. 64), My Best Salad Ever (p. 68), Halloumi Salad with Fresh Peas & Radishes (p. 107)

FUN FACT: This is a cheese to either barbecue or sear on a cast-iron pan.

HAVARTI (DENMARK)

MILK: Cow, pasteurized

FLAVOR: Mild, sweet, smooth

RECIPE: Smørrebrød & Salad (p. 44)

FUN FACT: Havarti can come in many different styles and flavors. I particularly love it on a burger.

KEFALOTYRI (GREECE)

MILK: Sheep, pasteurized

FLAVOR: Salty, sharp, bold

RECIPES: Greek Scrambled Eggs (p. 36), Superstar Greek Pastitsio (p. 119)

FUN FACT: Think of this like the pecorino of Greece. You may have to search to find it.

LA TUR (ITALY)

MILK: Goat, cow, and sheep blend, pasteurized

FLAVOR: Milky, funky, medium-bodied

RECIPE: The Ultimate Italian Cheese Board (p. 193)

FUN FACT: This Italian cheese is French-influenced, as it's made close to the French border.

LE DOUANIER (CANADA)

MILK: Cow, pasteurized

FLAVOR: Smooth, medium-bodied, slightly funky

RECIPE: Quebec Cheese Board (p. 181)

FUN FACT: This was made in honor of the famous French cheese Morbier (also featured in this book).

LOUIS D'OR (CANADA)

MILK: Cow, pasteurized

FLAVOR: Nutty, salty, sharp

RECIPE: Quebec Cheese Board (p. 181)

FUN FACT: This Quebec cheese is made in the alpine style like gruyère or Appenzeller.

MANCHEGO (SPAIN)

MILK: Sheep, pasteurized **FLAVOR:** Tangy, salty, sharp
RECIPES: Cheesy Spanish Omelet (p. 40), Spanish Fizz with 6-Month Aged Manchego (p. 161), Spanish Manchego Tasting (p. 178)
FUN FACT: Manchego is consumed by Don Quixote and his squire Sancho Panza in Miguel de Cervantes' famous novel *Don Quixote*, published in 1605.

MANGO GINGER STILTON (ENGLAND)

MILK: Cow, pasteurized
FLAVOR: Fruity, spicy, floral
RECIPE: After-Dinner English Cheese Board (p. 190)
FUN FACT: This is a bit of an acquired taste but super interesting as a dessert.

MIDNIGHT MOON (UNITED STATES & THE NETHERLANDS)

MILK: Goat, pasteurized
FLAVOR: Sweet, smooth, buttery
RECIPE: Uncle Sal's Bourbon Smash (p. 169)
FUN FACT: This cheese is #8 on my list of Top 13 Hidden-Gem Cheeses (p. 30).

MIMOLETTE (FRANCE)

MILK: Cow, pasteurized
FLAVOR: Salted caramel, nutty, extra sharp
RECIPE: All-French Cheese Board (p. 177)
FUN FACT: In an attempt to make a Dutch-style gouda, the French created Mimolette, which became one of the important cheeses in the country.

MOLITERNO TRUFFLE PECORINO (ITALY)

MILK: Sheep, pasteurized
FLAVOR: Salty, earthy, intense
RECIPE: The Ultimate Italian Cheese Board (p. 193)
FUN FACT: This cheese is infused with black truffle paste.

MORBIER (FRANCE)

MILK: Cow, unpasteurized
FLAVOR: Smooth, slightly funky, sharp
RECIPE: All-French Cheese Board (p. 177)
FUN FACT: The thin line of ash through the center separates morning and afternoon milk, as the cows feed on different things in the morning and night.

MOUNTAINOAK GOUDA, 3-YEAR AGED (CANADA)
MILK: Cow, pasteurized
FLAVOR: Nutty, salted caramel, umami
RECIPE: Ontario Cheese Board (p. 189)
FUN FACT: This cheese is lactose-free.

MOZZARELLA (ITALY)
MILK: Cow, pasteurized **FLAVOR:** Mild, firm, melty
RECIPE: Niagara-Inspired Stromboli (p. 112)
FUN FACT: The method to make mozzarella, where curds are heated and repeatedly stretched (a technique called "pasta filata") is what makes it such a supremely melty cheese.

OSSAU-IRATY (FRANCE)
MILK: Sheep, unpasteurized
FLAVOR: Smooth, semifirm, tangy
RECIPE: All-French Cheese Board (p. 177), My Turkish Family Künefe (p. 146)
FUN FACT: Made in the Pyrenees, this is a heavily Spanish-inspired cheese.

PANEER (INDIA)
MILK: Cow, pasteurized
FLAVOR: Mild, delicate, sweet
RECIPE: Cheese Boutique Insiders' Saag Paneer (p. 133)
FUN FACT: There aren't many cheeses made in India, but paneer is (and you can make it easily at home too). It appears in many Indian dishes worldwide.

PAPILLON NOIR ROQUEFORT (FRANCE)
MILK: Sheep, unpasteurized
FLAVOR: Salty, creamy, super tangy
RECIPE: All-French Cheese Board (p. 177)
FUN FACT: The bacteria injected into blue cheese is called *Penicillium roqueforti*.

PARMIGIANO-REGGIANO (ITALY)
MILK: Cow, unpasteurized **FLAVOR:** Nutty, sharp, umami
RECIPES: Simple Vegetarian Pasta (p. 104), 5-Cheese Mac & Cheese (p. 108), Modesta's Pasta e Ceci (p. 115), Gnocchi al Pomodoro (p. 130), Prosciutto Lovers with a Side of Cheese (p. 185), A Cheesy Butter Board (p. 186), The Ultimate Italian Cheese Board (p. 193)
FUN FACT: It takes almost 160 gallons of milk to make a single 85-pound wheel.

PECORINO ROMANO (ITALY)

MILK: Sheep, pasteurized **FLAVOR:** Salty, sharp, tangy

RECIPES: Simple Vegetarian Pasta (p. 104), Modesta's Pasta e Ceci (p. 115), Gnocchi al Pomodoro (p. 130)

FUN FACT: This super-versatile cheese is perfect for grating onto pasta, finishing a pizza, or shaving onto grilled vegetables.

PIAVE (ITALY)

MILK: Cow, pasteurized **FLAVOR:** Mild, salty, umami

RECIPE: Spritz O'Clock & Snacks (p. 182)

FUN FACT: Piave is made from the milk of cows that graze the Dolomite Mountains. The flavor of the cheese shifts subtly depending on whether it's made from summer or winter milk. I consider this cheese a cousin to Parmigiano-Reggiano.

PROVOLONE (ITALY)

MILK: Cow, pasteurized **FLAVOR:** Mild, salty, medium-bodied

RECIPES: Super Bowl Cincinnati Cheese Sandwich (p. 52), Grilled Provolone Asado (p. 63)

FUN FACT: The name "provolone" comes from the Neapolitan word *provola*, which means globe-shaped.

QUESO FRESCO (MEXICO)

MILK: Cow, pasteurized

FLAVOR: Delicate, fresh, mild

RECIPE: Beerita with Queso Fresco (p. 165)

FUN FACT: This is one of the most versatile cheeses made anywhere, in my opinion. It's great on tacos, seared in a skillet, or paired with tea in the morning.

RACLETTE (SWITZERLAND)

MILK: Cow, unpasteurized

FLAVOR: Melty, aromatic, funky

RECIPE: Raclette Supernova (p. 128)

FUN FACT: This melting cheese is best friends with potatoes.

REBLOCHON (FRANCE)

MILK: Cow, unpasteurized **FLAVOR:** Aromatic, creamy, mushroomy

RECIPE: Après-Ski Tartiflette (p. 103)

FUN FACT: The name of this cheese comes from "reblocher," which means to pinch a cow's udder again—referring to the practice of a second milking, which creates a richer, creamier cheese.

RED LEICESTER (ENGLAND)

MILK: Cow, pasteurized **FLAVOR:** Funky, bold, buttery

RECIPE: After-Dinner English Cheese Board (p. 190)

FUN FACT: Similar to cheddar but with a crumbly texture, Red Leicester gets its distinctive orange-red color from annatto extract (made from the seeds of the achiote tree).

RICOTTA (ITALY)

MILK: Cow, pasteurized

FLAVOR: Mild, fresh, delicate

RECIPE: Homemade Ricotta (p. 88), My Turkish Family Künefe (p. 146)

FUN FACT: Ricotta is made from whey—the watery byproduct of cheese making—so it isn't truly a cheese at all! Like paneer, it's also great to make at home.

RIOPELLE (CANADA)

MILK: Cow, unpasteurized

FLAVOR: Creamy, aromatic, earthy

RECIPE: Quebec Cheese Board (p. 181)

FUN FACT: This cheese is named after the artist Jean-Paul Riopelle. The image on this wheel's wrapper is one of his most famous paintings.

SAINT AGUR (FRANCE)

MILK: Cow, pasteurized

FLAVOR: Blue, buttery, perfectly salty

RECIPE: Maple, Bacon & Blue Cheese Cheeseball (p. 80)

FUN FACT: For people intimidated by blue cheese, try this one. It's not very aggressive or powerful.

SKI QUEEN (GJETOST) (NORWAY)

MILK: Goat, pasteurized

FLAVOR: Sweet, caramel, buttery

RECIPE: Gjetost Grilled Cheese (p. 71)

FUN FACT: It's made with whey—a sweet byproduct of cheese making.

SMOKED APPLEWOOD CHEDDAR (ENGLAND)

MILK: Cow, pasteurized

FLAVOR: Smoky, bold, intense

RECIPE: After-Dinner English Cheese Board (p. 190)

FUN FACT: Wheels of smoked applewood cheddar are often dusted with paprika to enhance their golden appearance.

STILTON (ENGLAND)

MILK: Cow, pasteurized

FLAVOR: Robust, sharp, aggressive in the best kind of way

RECIPES: English-Style Potted Cheese (p. 60); After-Dinner English Cheese Board (p. 190)

FUN FACT: Stilton cheese can be made only in one of three English counties: Derbyshire, Leicestershire, and Nottinghamshire. It is no longer made in the county of Stilton!

TALEGGIO (ITALY)

MILK: Cow, pasteurized

FLAVOR: Funky, creamy, aromatic

RECIPE: The Ultimate Italian Cheese Board (p. 193)

FUN FACT: This cheese has the texture of perfectly cooked medium-rare beef tenderloin.

WILDWOOD (CANADA)

MILK: Cow, unpasteurized

FLAVOR: Sharp, smooth, alpine style

RECIPE: Ontario Cheese Board (p. 189)

FUN FACT: In 2023, this cheese won for the best cheese made in Canada at the SIAL cheese awards.

A WHEEL OF MONTANA INTENSO
shown on an antique cheese probe

CHEESE SPOTLIGHT: BLEU D'ELIZABETH

#2 on Afrim's Top 13 Hidden-Gem Cheeses (p. 29)

AFRIM'S TOP 13 HIDDEN-GEM CHEESES

I could never choose my top, most favorite cheese (though Parmigiano-Reggiano is up there). But I do have a lot to say about cheeses that don't get the attention they deserve. Thirteen is my favorite number, so I put together this list. Some will be familiar to you; others might be brand new. Either way, take a moment to read about them, or even better, taste them at your local cheese shop or wherever your travels take you.

1 AFFIENATO ITALY

MILK: Sheep, unpasteurized

FLAVOR: Sharp, salty, earthy

FUN FACT: This famous Tuscan pecorino, made by only one producer, is rubbed in wildflower honey that grows on the farm, and then is rolled in grass from the farm. The sheep that produce the milk for this cheese are eating that grass too. This is the true meaning of local.

WHY I LOVE IT: My first cheese-making experience, when I was 21 years old, was the 3 months I spent working at this dairy, Il Forteto.

2 BLEU D'ELIZABETH CANADA

MILK: Cow, unpasteurized

FLAVOR: Salty, creamy, perfectly balanced

FUN FACT: This organic cheese, made at a church in Quebec by my mentor Jean Morin, was featured on my TV show, *Cheese: A Love Story*.

WHY I LOVE IT: This is the one blue cheese that I always tell people to have in their fridge. It's great on a cheese board and great to cook with.

3 CEOUR DE NEUFCHÂTEL FRANCE

MILK: Cow, unpasteurized

FLAVOR: Mushroomy, earthy, buttery

FUN FACT: During WWI, women in Normandy made this heart-shaped cheese for their husbands going to fight.

WHY I LOVE IT: I love a good, cheesy love story!

4 CHAOURCE FRANCE

MILK: Cow, pasteurized

FLAVOR: Creamy, funky, buttery

FUN FACT: Leave this cheese at room temperature for 4–6 hours for the ultimate experience.

WHY I LOVE IT: This cheese has three different textures—the bloomy outer rind, the milky cream inside the rind, and the crumbly feta-like texture in the center. This happens organically during the ripening process.

5 DÉLICE DE BOURGOGNE FRANCE

MILK: Cow, pasteurized

FLAVOR: Super creamy, buttery, salty

FUN FACT: Over the last 10 years, the production of this cheese has skyrocketed by almost 1,000 percent.

WHY I LOVE IT: It's uncomplicated, perfectly creamy, and fantastic spread on a baguette.

6 ÉPOISSES FRANCE

MILK: Cow, pasteurized

FLAVOR: Aromatic, strong, powerful

FUN FACT: It's illegal to have this on your person while traveling on public transportation in Paris—it's that stinky.

WHY I LOVE IT: The pungent, salty aggressiveness of this cheese is unforgettable.

7 MAHÓN SPAIN

MILK: Cow, pasteurized

FLAVOR: Salty, grassy, sharp

FUN FACT: This cheese comes from the isle of Menorca. Cows here eat grass that's coated in salt from the ocean, and their milk produces a naturally extra-salty cheese.

WHY I LOVE IT: The taste of ocean water that comes through in this cheese is unlike anything I've ever tasted.

8 MIDNIGHT MOON

UNITED STATES & THE NETHERLANDS

MILK: Goat, pasteurized

FLAVOR: Sweet, smooth, buttery

FUN FACT: This is a collaboration between Cypress Grove dairy in California and a Dutch cheese master.

WHY I LOVE IT: It's lactose-free and has a really interesting softness to the texture, even though it's a harder cheese.

9 MYZITHRA GREECE

MILK: Sheep, pasteurized

FLAVOR: Salty, tangy, sharp

FUN FACT: This cheese is best when grated onto pasta or drizzled with honey.

WHY I LOVE IT: It's great with pasta but is so different from the more traditional Italian cheeses I grew up eating.

10 PRIMA DONNA THE NETHERLANDS

MILK: Cow, pasteurized

FLAVOR: Fruity, nutty, smooth

FUN FACT: Think of this cheese as a hybrid of aged gouda and Parmigiano-Reggiano.

WHY I LOVE IT: It was one of the first cheeses I was introduced to when I used to go on cheese-sourcing trips with my dad. It's super nostalgic for me.

11 ROBIOLA ITALY

MILK: Blend of goat, sheep, and cow; pasteurized

FLAVOR: Delicate, milky, fresh

FUN FACT: Robiola made in Piedmont is highly French-influenced because of how close it's made to the border with France. The packaging lists ingredients in both French and Italian, which is rare.

WHY I LOVE IT: There are many different styles made all throughout Italy, but I love the one from Piedmont. It's made in the French brie style but with Italian milk.

12 SAINT-MAURE DE TOURAINE FRANCE

MILK: Goat, unpasteurized

FLAVOR: Barnyard, aromatic, pungent

FUN FACT: The authentic Saint-Maure is the one with the hay straw running through the center.

WHY I LOVE IT: The craftsmanship that goes into this cheese is inspiring. This is one of the most labor-intensive cheeses to make. It is made one by one in very small productions.

13 SÃO JORGE PORTUGAL

MILK: Cow, unpasteurized

FLAVOR: Grassy, salty, sharp

FUN FACT: This cheese is the pride of Portugal, the only European cheese-making country where the animals are grazing on grass 365 days a year.

WHY I LOVE IT: This is truly one of a kind because of how tied it is to the Portuguese terroir in the Azores.

CHEESE SPOTLIGHT: ROBIOLA

#11 on Afrim's Top 13 Hidden-Gem Cheeses (p. 30)

CHEESE SPOTLIGHT: PRIMA DONNA

#10 on Afrim's Top 13 Hidden-Gem Cheeses (p. 30)

Breakfast

With so many different styles of cheese made around the world, certain cheeses are meant to be enjoyed for breakfast. They're mild enough to gently wake up your palate in the morning, they're high in protein to give you energy for your day, and, let's be real: What's better than cheese, toast, and jam?

Open-Faced French Omelet

PREP TIME: 3 MINUTES **COOK TIME:** 7 MINUTES **SERVES:** 1

3 Tbsp salted butter

3 large eggs, beaten

Kosher salt

Freshly ground black pepper

Zest of ⅓ lemon

½ cup cream cheese

3½ oz (100 g) smoked salmon

2 Tbsp fresh dill, picked from stem, for garnish

2 Tbsp capers, drained, for garnish

Crusty baguette, for serving

1 glass chilled Burgundian Chablis, for serving (optional)

When I was in Paris filming *Cheese: A Love Story*, I had one day off when I could roam around the city to do whatever my heart desired. I knew immediately what I wanted to do. I wanted to have a beautiful lunch in a beautiful atmosphere, so I went to Fauchon. If you've had the good fortune to visit, then you know how magical this food shop is. I've been there a few times and I will always remember visiting it with my dad when I was a teenager to do reconnaissance and learn from the best. The cheeses, pastries, pantry items, cakes, breads, and cured meats were all stunning and top quality, and the merchandising and selection were perfect too. It was so clean that you could pretty much eat off the floor. Dad was a huge fan of this place and always tried to emulate certain aspects of it back home at Cheese Boutique in Toronto.

So I'm back there on my day off. I sit down and order the best omelet I've ever had, along with a perfectly chilled glass of Chablis. This recipe came about as a result.

1 In a 9-inch or 10-inch nonstick skillet over medium heat, melt the butter.

2 Pour the eggs into the skillet and cook for 3–4 minutes, or until the base forms a light crust.

3 Very gently, and using the largest spatula you have, flip the omelet over and smooth it out. Add a pinch each of salt and pepper and the lemon zest and cook for another 2 minutes.

4 Turn the heat down to low. Add dollops of cream cheese onto the omelet, then drape with smoked salmon.

5 Slide the omelet onto a plate and garnish with dill and capers. Serve with some crusty baguette and a glass of wine, if desired.

NOTE: This isn't your traditional-looking folded omelet. We're keeping this open. It should be the same diameter as the skillet you're using.

Greek Scrambled Eggs

PREP TIME: 5 MINUTES **COOK TIME:** 4 MINUTES **SERVES:** 2

4 large eggs

2½ oz (70 g) grated kefalotyri cheese

3 Tbsp salted butter

12 cherry tomatoes, halved

2 Tbsp finely chopped fresh oregano

3½ oz (100 g) Greek feta, crumbled, divided

Kosher salt

Freshly ground black pepper

2 pitas, warmed, for serving

Eggs and cheese are two humble ingredients that don't always get the love they deserve. They play off each other so well, and the possibilities of blending them in different recipes are endless. This recipe was inspired by my travels in Athens and a simple yet hearty breakfast that showcased typical Greek ingredients and high-quality local eggs. Sometimes you can't beat the classics.

1 Crack the eggs into a large mixing bowl and beat well to combine. Add the grated kefalotyri and stir again.

2 In a large nonstick skillet over medium heat, melt the butter.

3 Pour the eggs into the skillet and cook for about 2 minutes, then add the tomatoes, oregano, and three-quarters of the feta. Gently fold to combine.

4 Cook for another 1–2 minutes, or until the eggs are perfectly scrambled, then season with salt and pepper.

5 Divide the eggs onto 2 plates and top each portion with the remaining feta. Serve immediately alongside warm pita.

Late-for-Work Green Eggs

PREP TIME: 10 MINUTES **COOK TIME:** 15 MINUTES **SERVES:** 2

2 Tbsp extra virgin olive oil

3 green onions, finely chopped

1 clove garlic, finely chopped

1 tsp ground cumin

2 tsp ground coriander

1 tsp dried oregano

4 leaves black kale, roughly chopped

Juice of ½ lemon

1 cup baby spinach

½ cup fresh or frozen and thawed peas

Kosher salt

Freshly ground black pepper

4 large eggs

2 Tbsp roughly chopped fresh mint

2 Tbsp fresh dill

2½ oz (70 g) crumbled Greek feta

I'm not a big breakfast eater. I mean, who has the time in the morning to make a recipe like this? However, sometimes a recipe comes along that's worth the risk of being late for work. This is one of those recipes. It's hearty and healthy and packs a ton of flavor. My wife, Courtney, went on a kick with these kinds of Mediterranean-inspired breakfast dishes, and they immediately reminded me of the foods I grew up eating.

1 In a large nonstick skillet over medium-low heat, heat the olive oil. Add the green onions and garlic and cook until softened, 1–2 minutes.

2 Add the cumin, coriander, and oregano and stir well.

3 Add the kale and lemon juice and cook for about 3 minutes, stirring occasionally, until the kale has wilted. Add the spinach and peas and cook for another 1–2 minutes, stirring to wilt the spinach. Season with salt and pepper to taste.

4 With the back of a wooden spoon, make 4 small divots in the veggie mixture, then crack an egg into each divot. Cook for 2–3 minutes, uncovered, just until the whites start to set.

5 Cover the skillet and cook for another 2–3 minutes, until the whites are fully set but the yolks are still runny. Season with salt and pepper and scatter the mint, dill, and feta overtop. Serve immediately from the pan.

Cheesy Spanish Omelet

PREP TIME: 10 MINUTES **COOK TIME:** 50 MINUTES **SERVES:** 4

1 lb white potatoes

1 Tbsp extra virgin olive oil

1 cured chorizo sausage (mild or spicy), thinly sliced

1 red onion, sliced

1 red bell pepper, diced

2 cloves garlic, roughly chopped

16 cherry tomatoes, halved

8 large eggs

½ cup grated manchego (6-month aged is ideal)

¼ cup chopped fresh flatleaf parsley, plus more for garnish

Zest of 1 lemon

2 Tbsp salted butter

There are two things that I fell in love with during my many travels to Spain: the famous Spanish omelet and manchego cheese. Wherever you are in Spain, every restaurant has their own version of the Spanish omelet. It's a quick but satisfying bite, and though it doesn't traditionally include cheese, I thought I'd incorporate Spain's most popular cheese with its arguably most popular dish.

1 Preheat the oven to 350°F.

2 Place the potatoes in a steamer basket set over a pot of boiling water. Steam for 15–17 minutes, or until soft in the middle. Drain the potatoes and let them cool, then thinly slice them.

3 In a large cast-iron skillet over medium-high heat, heat the olive oil. Add the chorizo and cook until golden brown, 2–3 minutes, then transfer the chorizo to a bowl, leaving the rendered fat in the skillet.

4 Add the onions, peppers, and garlic to the skillet and cook, stirring occasionally, for 4–5 minutes. Add the cherry tomatoes and cook for 2 minutes, until softened. Transfer all the vegetables to the bowl with the chorizo and turn off the heat.

5 In a large bowl, whisk the eggs, then add the manchego, parsley, and lemon zest. Add the potatoes, chorizo, and vegetables and stir gently to combine.

6 Add the butter to the still-warm pan, swirl it around to coat the bottom, then pour in the omelet mixture.

7 Bake for 20 minutes, until the omelet is set and golden brown on top. Let sit for 5 minutes before cutting, then garnish with more parsley and serve.

NOTE: This recipe keeps beautifully in the fridge for a few days, so it's a great dish to make ahead for a weekend brunch or for a quick weekday breakfast or lunch.

ARRIVAL NETHERLANDS

Good Morning Dutch Quiche

PREP TIME: 10 MINUTES **COOK TIME:** 40 MINUTES **SERVES:** 4

1 premade 9-inch pie crust (see note)

6 large eggs

1 cup milk (any fat percentage)

½ cup shredded aged gouda

½ cup shredded aged beemster

½ cup diced country ham or prosciutto

¼ cup chopped green onions, plus more for garnish

¼ tsp kosher salt

¼ tsp freshly ground pepper

1 Tbsp fresh cilantro leaves, for garnish (optional)

I adore Dutch cheese, and I'm seemingly not alone. There's been a huge boom for it at my cheese shop in Toronto over the last few years. I'm finding that consumers love the big, bold, rich flavors of goudas and beemsters, and honestly, what's not to love? In the Netherlands, breakfast is a big deal and you'll find tons of phenomenal recipes for the most important meal of the day. This is a classic quiche, highlighting two cheeses that play a huge role in Dutch food culture.

1 Preheat the oven to 375°F.

2 If your pie crust doesn't come in an ovenproof baking dish (or if you want to make it look homemade!), place the pie dough in a 9-inch pie plate. Press it gently against the bottom and up the sides of the plate, and trim any excess crust if it hasn't been already crimped. Place the pie plate on a baking sheet in case the quiche bubbles over.

3 In a mixing bowl, whisk the eggs and milk until well combined. Add the gouda, beemster, ham, green onions, salt, and pepper and stir to combine.

4 Pour the egg mixture into the prepared pie crust, spreading it evenly.

5 Bake the quiche, still on the baking sheet, for 35–40 minutes, until the center is set and the top is golden brown.

6 Remove from the oven and let sit for 5 minutes before slicing and serving. Garnish with extra green onions and cilantro if desired.

NOTE: I like using good-quality store-bought pie crusts for this to save time without compromising on flavor, but you do you!

COPENHAGEN
DENMARK
DEPARTED

Smørrebrød & Salad

PREP TIME: 20 MINUTES **SERVES:** 4

FOR THE SALAD:

4 cups mixed salad greens

4 oz (115 g) havarti, cubed

1 large apple, thinly sliced

½ cup chopped walnuts

½ cup dried cranberries

Juice of ½ lemon

¼ cup extra virgin olive oil

Kosher salt

Freshly ground black pepper

FOR THE SMØRREBRØD:

2 Tbsp salted butter, room temperature

4 thin slices dark rye bread

4 slices havarti

2 Persian or baby cucumbers, thinly sliced

2 radishes, thinly sliced

Kosher salt

Freshly ground black pepper

2 Tbsp chopped fresh dill

Here's a two-part recipe that exemplifies a classic breakfast or brunch in Denmark. Smørrebrød is a traditional Danish open-faced sandwich that you can find different interpretations of across the country—it's that popular. Here, I'm using it to showcase another Danish classic: havarti cheese. Havarti comes in many different flavors and you can choose your favorite, but I recommend opting for the natural flavor and letting the simple ingredients shine.

1 To make the salad, in a large bowl, combine the salad greens, havarti, apples, walnuts, and cranberries. Set aside until ready to eat.

2 To make the smørrebrød, spread a thin layer of butter on each slice of rye bread. Top each slice with a piece of havarti, then add the sliced cucumbers, radishes, and salt and pepper. Garnish with a sprinkling of fresh dill.

3 Just before serving, drizzle the salad with the lemon juice and olive oil and toss gently to coat all the ingredients. Season with salt and pepper and serve immediately alongside the smørrebrød.

CHEESE SPOTLIGHT: TÊTE DE MOINE

shown on a girolle cheese cutter

Lunch

Around the world, lunch can mean many different things depending on where you are. In this chapter, you'll find dishes inspired by a filling, luxurious Mediterranean-style meal, as well as quick salads that are reminiscent of what you'd find in North America.

Normandy Baked Camembert

PREP TIME: 5 MINUTES **COOK TIME:** 12 MINUTES **SERVES:** 2–4

1 wheel (8 oz/225 g) raw-milk camembert

2 oz good-quality dry white wine (enjoy the rest of the bottle with lunch!)

3 sprigs fresh rosemary, halved

Honey, for garnish

Crusty baguette slices, for serving

On my travels in Normandy a few years back, I met up with chef Amir van Rooijen at his Michelin-starred restaurant Auberge du Vieux Puits, located in the historic town of Dieppe. In addition to playing tour guide—showing me the Canadian war memorial and the Dieppe food market—Chef Amir cooked some absolutely fantastic food for me. Normandy is known for its raw-milk, unpasteurized camembert, which comes in round wooden boxes, and it's fairly easy to find in North America at a good cheese shop or specialty food store.

1 Preheat the oven to 300°F.

2 Open the wooden camembert box, remove the wrapping from the cheese and the outside of the box (if there is any), and place the whole wheel back on the bottom side of the wooden container. Place the container on a baking sheet lined with parchment paper.

3 With a paring knife, pierce the top of the camembert in 6 spots to create small slits in the wheel.

4 Pour the white wine on top of the camembert and stick the rosemary sprigs into the slits in the cheese.

5 Bake the dressed cheese for 10–12 minutes, or until the cheese starts to soften and brown on top.

6 Remove the cheese from the oven, drizzle honey overtop, and serve immediately with some crusty baguette on the side.

Greek Bruschetta a.k.a. Dakos

PREP TIME: 5 MINUTES **SERVES:** 1

- 1 large field tomato, peeled
- 2–3 slices thick-cut, toasted sourdough bread
- ¼ cup crumbled Greek feta
- Freshly ground black pepper
- 1 pinch dried Greek oregano
- 1 Tbsp capers (optional)
- 3 tsp extra virgin olive oil
- 1 pinch fresh oregano leaves

I will never forget it. I was traveling from Athens to the ancient island of Crete, which seemed to take an eternity. It was pouring rain and I was super cranky, as I hadn't eaten and I was exhausted. When I arrived, I made my way to a beautiful family-run hotel called Enagron Ecotourism Village, and all the stress of the day just melted away. The innkeepers took me in quickly, got me a room, and told me to come down to the dining room for something to eat and drink. To this day, the meal they served me was one of the more memorable I've had. It was simple, refreshing, and super fresh.

A non-Cretan like me would say this dish is like a Greek version of bruschetta, but to a naturally born Cretan, this is dakos. Dakos is a traditional Cretan appetizer inspired by the beautiful ingredients that grow and are produced on the island: olive oil, tomatoes, capers, and, of course, cheese. My version of this dish, served for a quick but delicious lunch, will never be as good as theirs, but I hope it's close.

1. Set a strainer over a bowl. With a box cheese grater, grate the tomato into the strainer and allow the juices to drip into the bowl.
2. Spread the strained grated tomato over the bread slices and top with feta.
3. Sprinkle with pepper and dried oregano, and add the capers, if using.
4. Drizzle with olive oil and sprinkle with fresh oregano leaves and dig in.

NOTE: Because you're using so few ingredients here, buy the best quality that you can afford. And be sure to make this recipe when tomatoes are in season!

Super Bowl Cincinnati Cheese Sandwich

PREP TIME: 5 MINUTES **COOK TIME:** 4 MINUTES **SERVES:** 2

- 1 soft hoagie-style potato bun
- 3 slices Swiss gruyère
- 3 slices orange cheddar
- 3 slices smoked gouda
- 3 slices provolone
- 2 slices crispy cooked bacon
- 2 Tbsp good-quality store-bought caramelized onions
- 1 plum tomato, roughly chopped
- 5–6 crispy tortilla chips, crumbled
- 1 green onion, finely chopped
- Dill pickles, for serving

If a plate of nachos and a sandwich had a baby, it would look and taste something like this. In February 2022, just before Super Bowl LVI when the Cincinnati Bengals played the Los Angeles Rams, I was looking for something delicious, unhealthy, and fun to serve at a tailgate. This mash-up did the trick.

1 Preheat the oven to 350°F and line a baking sheet with parchment paper.

2 Cut open the potato bun lengthwise about three-quarters of the way through, keeping it attached along 1 seam.

3 Working with 1 cheese at a time, cover the top and bottom halves of the bun with overlapping cheese slices—you want it to look like an open-faced sandwich. Start with the gruyère, then add the cheddar, the gouda, and the provolone. Transfer the bun to the prepared baking sheet and bake for 3–4 minutes, or until the cheese is melted and creamy.

4 Transfer the bun to a serving plate. Add 1 slice of bacon to the top half of the bun and 1 to the bottom half.

5 Spread a line of caramelized onions down the middle of the bun, followed by the chopped tomatoes, crumbled tortilla chips, and green onions.

6 Sandwich the top and bottom buns together, then cut the sandwich in half. Serve each half with some dill pickles on the side.

Super Bowl Los Angeles Brie & Strawberries

PREP TIME: 5 MINUTES **SERVES:** 2

- 2 Tbsp extra virgin olive oil
- 4 tsp aged balsamic vinegar
- ¼ cup finely chopped fresh basil
- ¼ cup finely chopped fresh mint
- ¼ cup roughly chopped pistachios
- 2 Tbsp white sesame seeds
- Kosher salt
- Freshly ground black pepper
- 1 wheel (7 oz/200 g) vegan brie
- 3–4 strawberries
- ¼ cup fresh microgreens or baby arugula
- Crusty bread, for serving

This sequel recipe to the Super Bowl Cincinnati Cheese Sandwich (p. 52) is a healthier, lighter option with a California vibe. It represents the plant-based culture in Los Angeles and the Super Bowl LVI champs, the Los Angeles Rams. You can find plant-based brie at most retailers and fine cheese shops, but you can also keep it classic with a traditional French brie. Whichever style of brie you choose, make sure to leave it out at room temperature for 1 hour before serving.

1 In a medium mixing bowl, whisk the olive oil, balsamic vinegar, basil, mint, pistachios, sesame seeds, and salt and pepper to taste. Keep the whisk moving for about 1½ minutes to really bring the ingredients together and allow the herbs to release their flavors. You'll have a thick vinaigrette by the end.

2 Place the wheel of brie in the center of a serving platter.

3 Halve or slice the strawberries and arrange them around the brie. Give the vinaigrette a final whisk, then drizzle it over the brie and strawberries. Place the microgreens on top of the brie and serve with crusty bread.

Bufala & Peaches

PREP TIME: 35 MINUTES **SERVES:** 2

2 medium-ripe fresh peaches

¼ cup extra virgin olive oil

2½ Tbsp white balsamic vinegar

½ tsp flaky salt, plus more for serving

¼ tsp freshly ground black pepper

2 Tbsp roughly chopped hazelnuts

1 Tbsp chopped fresh tarragon

2 sprigs fresh thyme, leaves picked

1 ball (7 oz/200 g) bufala mozzarella

2 cups baby arugula

Crusty sourdough bread, for serving

This dish is inspired by the amazing women in my life: my mother, Modesta, who hails from Naples—the birthplace of mozzarella di bufala—and my wife, Courtney, who grew up in the Niagara region of Ontario, home to the best peaches in North America (if you ask me). This dish is a perfect August-through-September lunch, when bufala mozzarella and peaches are at their best. Now, with a dish this good comes certain responsibilities, so I suggest that you make this recipe only for your life partner or for your mother. They are the only two people who deserve it.

1 Cut the peaches into bite-sized pieces and place in a bowl for 30 minutes, or up to a few hours if you have the time. The natural juices will collect at the bottom of the bowl.

2 In a small bowl, whisk the olive oil, vinegar, salt, and pepper. Add the hazelnuts, tarragon, and thyme and whisk vigorously until the dressing thickens. Finally, add the collected peach juices to the vinaigrette.

3 Roughly tear the bufala mozzarella into pieces and place on a serving dish. Scatter the arugula overtop and around the cheese, then add the peaches.

4 Pour the vinaigrette on the salad and sprinkle flaky salt over the cheese pieces. Enjoy with crusty sourdough.

Philotimo
Organic
White Balsamic Vinegar

Parisian Green Bay Packers Soup

PREP TIME: 10 MINUTES **COOK TIME:** 30 MINUTES **SERVES:** 4

2 Tbsp salted butter

½ cup roughly chopped cooking onions

¼ cup diced carrots

¼ cup diced celery

⅓ cup all-purpose flour

½ tsp baking soda

2 cups whole milk

2 cups chicken stock

5 oz (140 g) Beaufort cheese, grated

5 oz (140 g) aged white Wisconsin cheddar, grated

2 tsp red pepper flakes

2 Tbsp finely chopped fresh flatleaf parsley

Crusty baguette, for serving

I can't resist a cheese soup, so when I see one on a menu, you can almost guarantee that I'll order it. This version is a bit of a hybrid, blending two very different cheeses—Beaufort from France and aged white cheddar from Wisconsin. Beaufort is an iconic French cheese known for its fruity, delicate alpine flavor, and it melts really well. Wisconsin is known for its dairy industry and punchy aged cheddar, of course, but you can't talk about Wisconsin without mentioning the Green Bay Packers. Here I give you my cheese soup inspired by people, places, and things that you might think don't go together, but in fact complement each other perfectly.

1 In a large saucepan or stockpot on medium heat, melt the butter. Add the onions, carrots, and celery and cook until tender, 3–4 minutes.

2 Sprinkle the flour over the vegetables and cook, stirring vigorously, for about 3 minutes or until the flour starts to bubble. Add the baking soda and stir to combine.

3 Gradually pour in the milk and chicken stock, stirring constantly, then bring to a boil over medium-high heat.

4 Once boiling, reduce the heat to low and simmer, stirring occasionally, until the soup thickens, 12–15 minutes.

5 Add the Beaufort and cheddar, stirring constantly to encourage even melting, then add the red pepper flakes.

6 Serve the soup topped with chopped fresh parsley and some crusty baguette on the side.

UNITED KINGDOM

English-Style Potted Cheese

PREP TIME: 5 MINUTES + SETTING **SERVES:** 4

- 7 oz (200 g) aged English cheddar
- 3½ oz (100 g) English stilton
- ⅓ cup salted butter, room temperature
- 2 Tbsp + 1 tsp good-quality port or red wine
- ¼ tsp mustard powder
- ¼ tsp freshly ground black pepper, plus more for garnish
- ¼ tsp Worcestershire sauce
- 1 pinch ground nutmeg
- 1 pinch smoked paprika
- 1–2 sprigs fresh thyme, leaves picked, plus more for garnish
- 1 box crackers (choose your favorite), for serving

Potted cheese is one of the coolest food ideas to come out of England. It's easy to make, you can add all sorts of ingredients, and it's perfect for entertaining—I like having it for lunch, but you can also serve this as an appetizer. I love making big batches to serve for Thanksgiving or Christmas, but if your holidays are like mine, things can get kind of chaotic and you might crave a quiet meal with a smaller group of loved ones. Potted cheese, a snowy afternoon, and *Home Alone* will hit the spot.

1 In a food processor, combine the cheddar, stilton, butter, port, mustard powder, pepper, Worcestershire, nutmeg, paprika, and thyme. Mix until smooth, stopping a few times to scrape down the sides of the bowl.

2 Transfer the mixture to a large bowl and refrigerate for at least 2 hours to set.

3 For serving, create individual portions in small ½-cup mason jars or little ramekins and let the cheese come up to room temperature for about 30 minutes. Sprinkle with black pepper and thyme leaves. Enjoy with crackers on the side.

NOTE: The potted cheese will keep, covered in the fridge, in mason jars for up to 2 weeks. Prior to eating, let the potted cheese sit at room temperature for 30 minutes.

Grilled Provolone Asado

PREP TIME: 2 MINUTES **COOK TIME:** 4 MINUTES **SERVES:** 2

5 oz (140 g) thinly sliced provolone

¼ cup all-purpose flour

1 tsp chopped fresh oregano, divided

1 tsp chopped fresh flatleaf parsley, divided

1 tsp chopped fresh tarragon, divided

1 tsp red pepper flakes, divided

Zest and juice of ½ lime

Crusty baguette slices, for serving

I've never been to Argentina, but visiting Buenos Aires is a dream of mine. And when I think of Argentine food, the first thing that comes to mind is an asado, a huge event where family and friends gather to barbecue a dazzling array of sausages, steaks, ribs, and many other meat proteins. This dish, called a provoleta, is typically served as an appetizer, but it's just as good for lunch. Melted cheese, fresh herbs, and lime—what could be better? Next time you're getting ready for an early-evening barbecue, channel Argentina and start the feast at lunchtime with this perfect crispy goodness.

1 Set your barbecue to medium-high heat, and place a cast-iron skillet on the grill to heat up. If you don't have access to a barbecue, place an oven-safe baking dish in the oven, and set the temperature to 400°F.

2 Neatly stack the provolone slices, then place the flour on a plate. Holding the stack of cheese, dip the top and bottom ends in the flour, then transfer to the hot cast-iron skillet or baking dish.

3 Sprinkle with half of the oregano, parsley, tarragon, and red pepper flakes and cook for 2 minutes, or until the bottom starts to brown.

4 If you're using the barbecue, carefully flip the cheese stack, keeping it intact, and close the barbecue lid. Cook for 2 minutes, until the second side has browned and the cheese begins to ooze. If you're using the oven, you don't need to flip the cheese stack—it will brown on its own during the 4 minutes of cooking time.

5 Sprinkle with the remaining herbs and red pepper flakes as well as the lime zest and juice. Serve immediately with crusty baguette slices.

Afrim & Courtney's Thai Halloumi Rice

PREP TIME: 5 MINUTES **COOK TIME:** 30 MINUTES **SERVES:** 3–4

1 cup riceberry rice

8 oz (225 g) halloumi, cut into ½-inch-thick pieces

1 can (19 oz) chickpeas, drained, rinsed, and dried

¼ cup extra virgin olive oil

1 tsp za'atar

Kosher salt

Freshly ground black pepper

Juice of 2 limes

⅓ cup fresh herbs (see note)

A few years ago, I was asked by a well-known Thai rice producer to come up with a few recipes that brought my Mediterranean background to their famous, beautiful Thai riceberry rice. If you haven't tried riceberry rice before, you're in for a treat. It's a whole-grain purple rice with a nutty, sweet flavor. And what goes better with sweet than salty? Bring on the halloumi! My amazing, supportive wife, Courtney, helped me come up with this ingredient pairing, and it's now one of our favorite meals to make together.

1 Preheat the oven to 375°F.

2 Place the rice in a pot and cover with lots of cold water. Swirl the rice around until the water is very cloudy, then pour out as much water as you can without losing any rice. Repeat until the water is mostly clear. Add 3 cups of room-temperature water to the pot and bring it to a simmer over medium heat.

3 Once the water is simmering, reduce the heat to low, cover the pot, and simmer very gently until the rice is tender and cooked through, about 20 minutes. Remove the pot from the heat and spread the cooked rice on a baking dish in an even layer.

4 Top the rice with halloumi slices and chickpeas, then drizzle the olive oil overtop. Sprinkle with za'atar and a pinch each of salt and pepper.

5 Bake the rice for 8 minutes, then set the oven to broil and place the baking dish on the top rack. Keep a very close eye on it!

6 Once the halloumi and chickpeas start to turn golden brown, 1–2 minutes, remove the baking dish from the oven and immediately drizzle the lime juice overtop.

7 Garnish with fresh herbs, and serve.

NOTE: You can use any fine fresh herbs you like. I use a mixture of cilantro, flatleaf parsley, and dill.

Marinated Mediterranean Feta

PREP TIME: 5 MINUTES **SERVES:** 2

½ cup extra virgin olive oil

¼ cup good-quality red wine vinegar

3–4 sprigs fresh rosemary

3–4 sprigs fresh thyme

3 bay leaves

2 Tbsp dried Greek oregano

1 tsp white sesame seeds

¼ tsp smoked paprika

¼ tsp sumac

¼ tsp freshly ground black pepper

1 piece (8 oz/225 g) Greek feta

Feta is one of my all-time fave cheeses—I grew up on it. When I was sick as a kid, my parents would give me chamomile tea, feta, and toast. This, they said, would cure any illness. I believed them, and even if that meal didn't quite heal me, it sure tasted good and put a smile on my face. My dad's family is from all over the Mediterranean: Turkey, Albania, Italy, and France. Feta is a commonly used ingredient in all those countries and cuisines, so I decided to highlight it with other superstar Mediterranean flavors in this versatile lunch dish. Serve it over salad, on toast, or with some tomatoes and cucumbers, or use it for that feta pasta dish that went viral on TikTok back in 2020.

1 In a resealable container or a wide-mouthed glass mason jar, combine all the ingredients except the feta. Whisk or shake well to combine.

2 Add the feta to the container, making sure it's completely submerged in the marinade.

3 Let the feta sit at room temperature for 1 hour to absorb the flavors, then serve with some of the marinade drizzled overtop. Store any remaining feta in the fridge for up to 3 weeks, making sure it's completely submerged.

NOTE: When you finish the feta, you can reuse the marinade for one more piece!

My Best Salad Ever

PREP TIME: 5 MINUTES **COOK TIME:** 5 MINUTES **SERVES:** 3–4

FOR THE DRESSING:

3 Tbsp extra virgin olive oil

2 Tbsp red wine vinegar

2 Tbsp roughly chopped unsalted pistachios

2 sprigs fresh thyme, leaves picked

Kosher salt

Freshly ground black pepper

FOR THE GRAPES:

1 Tbsp extra virgin olive oil

1 cup halved seedless green grapes

Kosher salt

Freshly ground black pepper

7 oz (200 g) halloumi, cut into ¾-inch-thick pieces

1 package (5 oz) arugula

This simple, unique salad is one of my favorite recipes in this entire book. It's my go-to for entertaining or when I'm doing a cooking demo for a big crowd, but it's also perfect for a quick but filling lunch at home. It doesn't call for many ingredients, so buy the best you can afford and transport yourself to a breezy lunch spot overlooking the Mediterranean.

1 To make the dressing, in a small mixing bowl, combine the olive oil, vinegar, and pistachios and stir to incorporate. Add the thyme, and the salt and pepper to taste, and stir again. Set aside.

2 To make the grapes, in a medium nonstick skillet over medium heat, warm the olive oil, then add the grapes. Season to taste with salt and pepper. Cook, stirring occasionally, for about 3 minutes, until the grapes start to caramelize and turn light golden brown. Transfer the grapes to a baking sheet to cool slightly.

3 Return the pan to the stove, turn the heat to high, and add the halloumi slices. Cook for about 1½ minutes, until the bottom is golden brown, then flip and cook for another minute, or until the second side is browned as well. Remove the pan from the heat.

4 Scatter the arugula over a large serving plate and add the halloumi slices and cooked grapes overtop. Give the dressing another good stir to re-emulsify it, then drizzle it over the salad and enjoy immediately.

Gjetost Grilled Cheese

PREP TIME: 5 MINUTES **COOK TIME:** 8 MINUTES **SERVES:** 2

4 slices crusty sourdough or your favorite bread

Salted butter, room temperature

3½ oz (100 g) Ski Queen (gjetost) cheese, thinly sliced

1 pear, sliced

Whether you call it gjetost, brunost, or simply Norwegian brown cheese, this dairy product is Norway's most famous cheesy export. It can be made with cow's or goat's milk, and it looks and tastes like a rich caramel. It's one of those "if you know, you know" types of foods. Allow me to introduce you!

1 Place a nonstick skillet over medium heat. Butter 1 side of each bread slice.

2 Lay 2 slices of bread, butter side down, in the skillet. Layer the gjetost on top of the bread slices, then close up the sandwiches with the remaining bread slices, butter side up.

3 Cook for 3–4 minutes per side, until the bread is golden brown and the cheese has melted.

4 Remove the cooked sandwiches from the skillet and let them cool for 1 minute, then cut on a diagonal and enjoy with sliced pear on the side.

Croque Monsieur

PREP TIME: 5 MINUTES **COOK TIME:** 15 MINUTES **SERVES:** 2

FOR THE BÉCHAMEL SAUCE:

1 Tbsp salted butter

1 Tbsp all-purpose flour

¾ cup milk

Kosher salt

Freshly ground black pepper

Ground nutmeg, to taste

FOR THE SANDWICHES:

4 slices sourdough bread

2 Tbsp Dijon mustard

4 slices cooked ham (jambon de Paris or prosciutto cotto)

¾ cup grated Comté

2 Tbsp salted butter

Many years ago, on a cheese inspiration trip in the Loire Valley, I found myself in the town of Amboise after a crazy-long travel day. One of those planes, trains, and automobiles type of days. I was exhausted and starving past the point of being "hangry." I stopped into a tiny local bistro and had one of the best food experiences of my life—a perfect croque monsieur. I can't be certain if it was perfect because I was so hungry or because the sandwich was so damn good, but either way, this French classic rocks and I hope you enjoy it.

1 Preheat the oven to 350°F.

2 To make the béchamel sauce, in a saucepan over medium heat, melt the butter. Add the flour and cook for a few minutes, stirring constantly, to create a roux. Gradually whisk in the milk, and continue to whisk until the mixture thickens and becomes smooth. Season with salt, pepper, and nutmeg to taste, and set aside.

3 To assemble the sandwiches, lay out 2 slices of bread and spread a thin layer of Dijon on each. Place 2 pieces of ham on each slice, then top with a generous amount of Comté. Close up the sandwiches with the remaining 2 slices of bread.

4 Heat a large nonstick skillet over medium heat, then add the butter to melt. While the butter melts, dip each sandwich in the saucepan with the béchamel, making sure both sides are well coated. This can get a bit messy, but it's worth it!

5 Place the sandwiches in the skillet and cook for 2–3 minutes per side, just to start the browning and melting process, then transfer the sandwiches to a baking sheet.

6 Bake the sandwiches in the oven for 5–7 minutes, until heated through and slightly crispy on top. Let cool for a minute, then cut in half and serve.

NOTE: For you brunch fans, add a fried egg on top of the sandwich to make the equally classic and famous croque madame.

Bougie Euro-Style Grilled Cheese

PREP TIME: 2 MINUTES **COOK TIME:** 9 MINUTES **SERVES:** 1

5 slices Swiss gruyère (see note)

2 thick slices multigrain sourdough bread

¼ cup salted butter (ideally 84% milk fat), divided

It's taken me years to do, but I feel I have really mastered the grilled cheese sandwich. This recipe includes a few little tricks and tips you can use to improve your grilled cheese game at home, but the first step is in the shopping and ingredient preparation. Because there are so few ingredients in a grilled cheese, my advice is to buy the best-quality bread, butter, and cheese that you can afford. And don't rush the process. You'll find that you feel fancy and nostalgic all at the same time.

1 Layer 4 slices of gruyère on a piece of bread, trying to cover as much surface area as possible. Break up the final slice and place it wherever the bread is peeking through—every inch should be covered. Top with the remaining slice of bread.

2 In a nonstick pan over medium heat, slowly melt about three-quarters of the butter. High-quality butter will start to foam, and once that happens, place the sandwich in the pan and turn the heat to just above medium but not quite medium-high. Move the sandwich around the pan so it absorbs the butter.

3 Apply a bit of pressure to the top of the sandwich so it gets a golden-brown crust—you could do this with your spatula or rest a small pot on top of the sandwich. After 4–5 minutes, you should have a perfectly browned sandwich bottom.

4 Remove the sandwich from the pan, turn the heat back down to medium, and add the remaining butter. Once the butter foams up, return the sandwich to the pan, uncooked side down. Move it around so it absorbs the butter and apply pressure once again. Cook for 3–4 minutes on the second side, until perfectly golden brown.

5 Transfer the sandwich to a cutting board and let it rest for 1½ minutes before slicing in half. I know this sounds a bit annoying, but I promise, this is the ideal resting time. Dig in.

NOTE: Buy high-quality gruyère that has been sliced fresh and not prepackaged. And let the cheese sit out at room temperature for 2 hours before preparing the sandwich.

Appetizers

Cheese can be the ultimate snacking food, and a cheesy appetizer is perfect to get your palate ready for the main course. Here are some appetizers that are as versatile as they are delicious.

ARRIVAL NETHERLANDS

Beemster & Onion Tarts

PREP TIME: 15 MINUTES **COOK TIME:** 50 MINUTES **SERVES:** 4

- 1 sheet frozen all-butter puff pastry, thawed
- 2 Tbsp salted butter
- 1 Tbsp extra virgin olive oil
- 2 large onions, thinly sliced
- 1 Tbsp balsamic vinegar
- 1 tsp sugar
- Kosher salt
- Freshly ground black pepper
- 4 oz (115 g) beemster, grated
- Fresh thyme leaves, for garnish

Puff pastry is so simple, yet impactful, and this recipe is a perfect starter that will impress your friends and yourself! It balances big, complex cheesy flavors with sweetness from the caramelized onions, and you can tailor it to the type of aged beemster that suits you. The older the beemster, the bigger the flavor.

1 Preheat the oven to 400°F and line a baking sheet with parchment paper.

2 On a lightly floured surface, roll out the puff pastry sheet to about ¼ inch thick. Cut the pastry into smaller 4- or 5-inch squares or circles. Place the pastry squares or circles on the prepared baking sheet and refrigerate while you caramelize the onions.

3 In a large skillet over medium heat, heat the butter and olive oil. Add the sliced onions and sauté until they start to soften, about 5 minutes. Reduce the heat to low and continue cooking the onions, stirring occasionally, until they caramelize and turn golden brown, 20–25 minutes.

4 Stir in the balsamic vinegar and sugar and cook for an additional 2–3 minutes, until the flavors meld together. Season with salt and pepper.

5 Remove the pastry from the fridge. Spoon a generous amount of the caramelized onions on each piece of pastry, leaving a small border around the edges.

6 Sprinkle the grated beemster evenly over the onions on each tart.

7 Bake the tarts for 15–18 minutes, or until the pastry is golden brown and the cheese has melted.

8 Remove the tarts from the oven and let them cool for a few minutes. Garnish with fresh thyme leaves before serving.

Maple, Bacon & Blue Cheese Cheeseball

PREP TIME: 15 MINUTES + CHILLING **SERVES:** 4

- 2 cups mild blue cheese (see note)
- 1 cup cream cheese
- 3 Tbsp maple syrup
- 2 tsp salted butter, room temperature
- 1 cup crispy bacon bits (homemade or store-bought), divided
- ¼ cup caramelized onion jam
- 3 sprigs fresh thyme, leaves picked
- ¼ cup chopped walnuts
- Freshly ground black pepper
- Rye crackers, for serving
- Sliced pear, for serving

The first time I ever had a cheeseball was when I was visiting family in Pennsylvania many years ago. To this day, the cheeseball is looked at as an old-fashioned dinner appetizer, reminiscent of shag carpeting and retro tackiness. Yeah, well, so what? It's awesome, and I'm ready to embrace this American culinary classic and make it my own with some Canadian flavors.

1 In a large bowl, combine the blue cheese, cream cheese, maple syrup, and butter. Mix well with a wooden spoon until the ingredients come together in an even paste.

2 Stir in ½ cup of bacon bits, the caramelized onion jam, and the thyme, then place the bowl in the fridge to chill for at least 1 hour.

3 Once the cheese mixture is cold and easy to handle, quickly roll it into a ball shape.

4 Sprinkle the remaining ½ cup bacon bits and the chopped walnuts on a plate and mix with your fingers. Season with freshly ground black pepper. Roll the cheeseball in the bacon bits, walnuts, and pepper until it's fully coated.

5 Let the cheeseball come to room temperature before serving, then transfer it to a nice plate and place rye crackers and sliced pears on the side.

NOTE: I like Saint Agur or Cambozola for the blue cheese here, but use what you prefer.

ARRIVAL NETHERLANDS

Kaaskroketten or Dutch-Style Crispy Croquettes

PREP TIME: 20 MINUTES **COOK TIME:** 10 MINUTES **SERVES:** 2–3

2 cups cooked mashed potatoes

1 cup grated aged beemster

2 Tbsp chopped fresh flatleaf parsley

2 large eggs, divided

Kosher salt

Freshly ground black pepper

½ cup all-purpose flour

1 cup breadcrumbs

Vegetable oil, for frying

Lemon wedge, for serving

Garlic mayo, for dipping

I'm a bit of a sucker for crispy croquettes. These Dutch kaaskroketten are super tasty and the perfect appetizers. This is one of those recipes that your guests will hoover down quickly, so if you don't want to share these, I totally get it. Sometimes being selfish is important. I like to use the oldest beemster I can for these, and I encourage you to do the same. A 12- to 18-month aged beemster is naturally complex, and when heated up this way, the flavor profile is intense and awesome.

1 In a mixing bowl, combine the mashed potatoes, beemster, parsley, 1 egg, and a pinch each of salt and pepper.

2 Shape the mixture into small croquettes or cylinders, 2–3 inches long.

3 Set up a breading station with separate bowls: one with the flour, one with the remaining beaten egg, and one with the breadcrumbs.

4 Roll each croquette in flour, dip it in beaten egg, and coat it evenly with breadcrumbs, then set it aside on a baking sheet. Repeat until all your croquettes are breaded.

5 Meanwhile, in a Dutch oven over medium-high heat, heat 3–4 inches of vegetable oil to about 350°F. To test if it's ready, place the handle of a wooden spoon in the oil. If bubbles form around the handle, the oil is hot enough.

6 Working in batches, use a slotted spoon to gently lower a few croquettes into the oil. Make sure not to overcrowd the pan. Fry the croquettes until golden brown and crispy, 4–5 minutes.

7 Remove the croquettes from the oil with a slotted spoon and place them on a plate lined with paper towel to drain excess oil. Season with a pinch of salt, let cool for 1 minute, then serve immediately with a lemon wedge and some garlic mayo on the side.

ITALY
DEPARTED

Bougie Burrata

PREP TIME: 5 MINUTES **SERVES:** 4

2 balls (each 4 oz/115 g) burrata, room temperature

2 cups baby arugula

1 cup microgreens of your choosing

1½ Tbsp extra virgin olive oil

3 tsp aged balsamic vinegar

Flaky salt

1 tin (1 oz) caviar

2 Tbsp finely chopped fresh chives, for garnish

Thinly sliced sourdough bread, toasted, for serving

Champagne, for serving (optional)

Years ago, I did an event with my friend and seafood culinary genius, Chef Ned Bell, out in Vancouver. Together we created a dinner menu to debunk the myth that cheese and seafood don't work well together. We served six amazing dishes to a sold-out crowd of ninety people at the Vancouver Aquarium, and I still remember it as one of the coolest, most unique dinners I've ever participated in. How often do you get to drink champagne and eat caviar next to a shark tank? This is an expensive recipe, so bust it out for someone you love or for a special occasion.

1 Place the burrata balls on a serving platter. Using a paring knife, make a shallow slit from one end of the burrata ball to the other, then gently open the burrata to reveal the creamy interior.

2 Scatter the arugula around the burrata, then add the microgreens on top.

3 Drizzle the olive oil inside the burrata and over the greens. Repeat with the balsamic vinegar, drizzling it mostly inside of the burrata with just a touch on the greens.

4 Add a small pinch of flaky salt to the burrata, but keep it small, as the caviar will add a lot of saltiness.

5 Add a good dollop of caviar to the center of the burrata and garnish with chives. Serve immediately with toasted sourdough, and champagne, if desired.

Nick's Burrata & Peas

PREP TIME: 10 MINUTES **COOK TIME:** 2 MINUTES **SERVES:** 2

- 1 cup shelled fresh peas
- 2 Tbsp aged balsamic vinegar
- 2 Tbsp extra virgin olive oil
- ¼ cup roughly chopped Marcona almonds
- Kosher salt
- Freshly ground black pepper
- 2 cups mixed salad greens
- ¼ cup fresh mint leaves, chopped
- ¼ cup fresh basil leaves, chopped
- 1 ball (7 oz/200 g) burrata
- Crusty baguette, for serving

For certain occasions, we'll close down Cheese Boutique for an "after-hours" dinner. Some years back, my close friend Nick was celebrating his fiftieth birthday, and we put together a six-course tasting menu with wine pairings for him and his guests. I pulled out all the stops, but this simple appetizer was the birthday boy's favorite dish. As a present, I promised to name the recipe after him. It's ideal in the summer, when peas are in season.

1 Start by blanching the fresh peas. Bring a pot of salted water to a boil. Add the fresh peas and cook for about 2 minutes, until they are bright green and tender-crisp. Immediately drain the peas and transfer them to a bowl of ice water to stop the cooking process. Drain the peas again and set aside.

2 In a small bowl, whisk the balsamic vinegar, olive oil, Marcona almonds, salt, and pepper.

3 Arrange the salad greens, mint, and basil on a serving platter. Gently tear open the burrata ball and place it in the center of the salad greens. Scatter the blanched peas over the greens and on top of the burrata, then drizzle the dressing over the cheese and salad, making sure to coat the greens and peas evenly. Serve right away with some crusty baguette.

ITALY
DEPARTED

Homemade Ricotta

PREP TIME: 10 MINUTES + DRAINING **COOK TIME:** 45 MINUTES **MAKES:** 1 LB (450 G)

4 cups whole milk (see note)

1 cup heavy cream

½ tsp kosher salt

3 Tbsp fresh lemon juice

I think ricotta is an undervalued cheese. Yes, it's mild and simple, but it's also the one cheese that you can make and master from your home, fairly easily. It's low risk but high reward, and there are so many ways to enjoy it. Once you see how simple it is, you may never want store-bought ricotta again!

1 Place a fine-mesh strainer over a large pot, then line the strainer with a double layer of cheesecloth, making sure there's enough overhang to gather up the cloth later.

2 In a separate large pot, combine the milk, cream, and salt. Cook over medium heat, stirring occasionally to prevent scorching, until it reaches 190°F. You need a cooking thermometer here to monitor the temperature.

3 Remove the pot from the heat and gently stir in the lemon juice. Let the mixture sit undisturbed for 5–10 minutes. During this time, curds will begin to form as the acid reacts with the milk proteins. After 5–10 minutes, the mixture will have separated into curds (solids) and whey (liquid). Carefully ladle the curds into the prepared cheesecloth-lined strainer.

4 Allow the curds to drain for 15–25 minutes, then lift the edges of the cheesecloth and gather the curds gently. Tie the ends of the cheesecloth to create a pouch, then hang the pouch from the faucet over the sink or place it over a bowl to allow the remaining whey to drip out. Let the ricotta hang for 1–2 hours more, or until it reaches your desired consistency. The longer it drains, the drier the ricotta will become, so adjust as your recipe dictates.

5 Once the ricotta reaches your preferred texture, transfer it to an airtight container and refrigerate. It's best used within 3–4 days. Congratulations—you are officially a cheese maker. Welcome to the club.

NOTE: For both the milk and the cream, get the full-fat stuff. Try and source the milk and cream from a reputable, high-end local dairy as well. Using great milk to start off will make the biggest difference in the world here.

Sweet Whipped Ricotta

PREP TIME: 15 MINUTES **SERVES:** 4–6

1 cup Homemade Ricotta (p. 88), room temperature

2 Tbsp extra virgin olive oil

2 Tbsp wildflower honey

1 tsp vanilla extract

Zest of 2 oranges

2 Tbsp finely chopped fresh mint

Kosher salt

FOR SERVING:

Carrot sticks

Celery sticks

Cucumber spears

Quartered radishes

Pitas

Breadsticks

1 In a blender or food processor, combine the ricotta, olive oil, honey, vanilla, orange zest, mint, and a pinch of salt. Blend the ingredients on medium-high speed until the mixture becomes super smooth and creamy. Stop and scrape down the sides of the blender or food processor, if needed. If a blender scares you, you can make this the old-fashioned way, with a fork, a bowl, and some muscle.

2 Taste and adjust the sweetness or seasoning by adding more honey, salt, or any of the other flavorings you prefer.

3 Once the mixture is creamy and well combined, transfer it to a serving bowl. You can serve the whipped ricotta immediately or cover and refrigerate for up to 2 hours to let the flavors meld and the mixture slightly firm up.

4 Serve the whipped ricotta with fresh, crunchy vegetables, pitas, and breadsticks. Store any leftovers in an airtight container in the fridge for up to 5 days.

ITALY

Savory Whipped Ricotta

PREP TIME: 15 MINUTES **SERVES:** 4–6

1 cup Homemade Ricotta (p. 88), room temperature

2 Tbsp extra virgin olive oil, plus more for serving

1 clove garlic, minced

1 tsp fresh lemon juice

2 Tbsp chopped fresh basil

1 Tbsp chopped fresh rosemary

¼ cup chopped olives (any kind)

¼ cup chopped sun-dried tomatoes

1 pinch red pepper flakes (optional)

Kosher salt

Freshly ground black pepper

FOR SERVING:

Toasted baguette slices

Toasted focaccia

Crackers

Carrot sticks

Celery sticks

1 In a food processor, combine the ricotta, olive oil, garlic, lemon juice, chopped herbs, olives, sun-dried tomatoes, and red pepper flakes. Mix until smooth and creamy. You can adjust the consistency by adding lemon juice to thin it out or olive oil to help thicken to your preference. Season with salt and pepper.

2 Once the mixture is well combined and creamy, transfer it to a serving bowl. Before serving, drizzle a little extra olive oil on top or sprinkle with optional toppings for presentation (red pepper flakes, chopped olives, and chopped sun-dried tomatoes would all look beautiful).

3 Serve the savory whipped ricotta with toasted baguette and focaccia slices, crackers, and fresh crunchy carrot and celery sticks, or use it as a spread for sandwiches. Store any leftovers in an airtight container in the fridge for up to 5 days.

SWEET WHIPPED RICOTTA (p. 90)

SAVORY WHIPPED RICOTTA (p. 91)

Ronaldo's Cod Fritters

PREP TIME: 30 MINUTES + SOAKING **COOK TIME:** 20 MINUTES **SERVES:** 4

7 oz (200 g) salted codfish (also called bacalhau; see note)

2 Yukon Gold potatoes

3½ oz (100 g) mozzarella, grated

Olive oil, for frying

1 small onion, finely chopped

2 cloves garlic, minced

¼ cup chopped fresh flatleaf parsley

2 large eggs, beaten

Kosher salt

Freshly ground black pepper

Lemon wedge, for serving

Garlic mayo, for dipping

NOTE: If soaking your own bacalhau doesn't sound like a project you want to take on, you can often find it presoaked and shredded at Portuguese grocery stores.

A chef buddy of mine in New York was the personal chef to soccer superstar Cristiano Ronaldo and his family. For obvious reasons, Ronaldo was very serious about his diet and the food he puts into his body—look at the guy, he's the epitome of health and success. However, occasionally he liked to indulge, and he'd ask my buddy to make these cod fritters. It was a snack that reminded him of his hometown in Portugal. So this recipe is for all the athletes and diet-conscious people out there. It's the ultimate snack for your cheat day. Although the star of this dish is the cod, the mozzarella brings all the other flavors together.

1 Start by soaking the salted codfish in cold water for 24 hours, changing the water several times to remove the excess salt. After soaking, drain the codfish and remove any skin or bones, then shred the flesh into small pieces. Set aside.

2 Peel the potatoes and cut them into chunks. Bring a large pot of salted water to a boil over high heat, add the potatoes, and cook until tender, 8–10 minutes.

3 Drain the potatoes, return them to the pot, and mash them while still hot. You want the potatoes as smooth as possible. Add the grated mozzarella and mix to combine.

4 In a medium skillet over medium heat, heat 1 tablespoon olive oil. Sauté the onions and garlic until the onions are soft and translucent, then remove from the heat.

5 In a large bowl, combine the shredded codfish, cheesy mashed potatoes, sautéed onions and garlic, parsley, and eggs. Season with a pinch each of salt and pepper, but remember that the fish is very salty, so don't overdo it.

6 Using your hands, shape the mixture into small oval or round fritters, and set aside on a baking sheet.

7 Meanwhile, in a deep skillet over medium-high heat, heat about 2 inches of oil. To test if the oil is hot enough, place the handle of a wooden spoon in the oil. If it bubbles up around the handle, the oil is ready.

8 Working in batches, carefully place the fritters into the hot oil and fry them until they are golden brown and crispy on all sides, about 4 minutes total.

9 Remove the fritters with a slotted spoon and place them on a plate lined with paper towel to drain the excess oil. Serve while still hot with a squeeze of lemon juice and some garlic mayo for dipping.

Canadiana Baked Brie

PREP TIME: 5 MINUTES **COOK TIME:** 15 MINUTES **SERVES:** 2–4

1 wheel (8 oz/225 g) Canadian brie

4 slices good-quality bacon, diced

5 Tbsp maple syrup

¼ cup roughly chopped pecans

1 box plain crackers

Who doesn't love a baked brie? The options and flavors are limitless (see my Wednesday-Night Baked Brie on p. 99 for a completely different take). This version is super fun and super easy. It showcases ingredients that we are very well known for in Canada. The only thing that could make this more Canadian is if you eat it while watching *Deadpool* (I love Ryan Reynolds). I know baked brie is typically a holiday recipe, but with readily available ingredients like these, you can make this all year round.

1 Preheat the oven to 375°F.

2 Place your brie into an ovenproof dish, ideally something that closely fits the brie—you don't want a massive casserole dish for this.

3 Score entire top surface of the brie, so the maple syrup can seep in later.

4 Bake the brie for about 12 minutes, until it starts to brown.

5 Meanwhile, place the diced bacon in a dry sauté pan and cook on medium heat until almost crispy, 5–6 minutes. Transfer the bacon to a plate lined with paper towel to drain excess oil.

6 Return the bacon to the pan, then add the maple syrup and pecans. Cook for another 3 minutes to incorporate the flavors.

7 Once the baked brie is out of the oven, top it with the maple-pecan-bacon mixture. Eat immediately with your favorite crackers.

Wednesday-Night Baked Brie

PREP TIME: 5 MINUTES **COOK TIME:** 12 MINUTES **SERVES:** 2–4

1 wheel (8 oz/225 g) Canadian brie

½ cup good-quality raspberry or blueberry jam

¼ cup crushed almonds (if you can find Marcona almonds, use those)

2 sprigs fresh rosemary, leaves roughly chopped

1 baguette, sliced and toasted

I hate pigeonholing baked brie as a holiday food. This version is easy, comforting, and a great way to use up the ingredients you find in your fridge on a random Wednesday when your friends stop by at the last minute. I promise, once you make this, you'll find yourself making it every other night of the week as well.

1 Preheat the oven to 375°F.

2 Place your brie in an ovenproof dish, ideally something that closely fits the brie—you don't want a massive casserole dish for this.

3 Score the entire top surface of the brie, so the jam can seep in. Spread the jam liberally overtop, then cover with the crushed almonds.

4 Bake the brie for 6 minutes, then remove it from the oven and top with the rosemary. Bake for an additional 6 minutes, or until the cheese starts to ooze out. Remove from the oven and serve immediately with toasted baguette.

CHEESE SPOTLIGHT: MYZITHRA

#9 in Afrim's Top 13 Hidden-Gem Cheeses (p. 30)

Dinner

No matter where you find yourself in the world, the evening meal is one to savor. It's where flavors shine and memories are made, and what's a dreamy memory without cheese? However, watch your portion control—too much cheese eaten at night can apparently cause nightmares. Don't believe me? Look it up.

FRANCE

Après-Ski Tartiflette

PREP TIME: 10 MINUTES **COOK TIME:** 40 MINUTES **SERVES:** 6–8 + LEFTOVERS

3 lb Yukon Gold potatoes, skin left on, sliced into ⅓-inch disks

10½ oz (300 g) bacon, cubed

2 Tbsp salted butter

1 yellow onion, thinly sliced

1 clove garlic, minced

½ cup dry white wine

Kosher salt

Freshly ground black pepper

½ cup heavy cream

1 lb (450 g) Reblochon cheese, cut into small wedges

Tartiflette is a dish I find myself craving almost daily in the winter. It's the perfect comfort food—essentially potatoes, bacon, onions, and cheese—and in the French Alps is often served alongside a steak and some roasted vegetables. What could be better after a day on the slopes? But even if, like me, you are not quite the skiing type, this is just good, honest food that can be enjoyed no matter where you are.

1 Preheat the oven to 400°F and bring a large pot of salted water to a boil over high heat.

2 Parboil the potatoes for 6–7 minutes, until they're almost cooked but not quite—you want them holding their shape. Drain the potatoes and set them aside to cool.

3 Heat a large skillet over medium heat and fry the bacon cubes until almost crispy, 3–4 minutes.

4 Discard half of the bacon fat, then add the butter, onions, and garlic to the bacon. Cook for 3–4 minutes, or until the onions are golden brown.

5 Deglaze the skillet with the white wine and continue to cook until most of the liquid has evaporated, then set the pan aside.

6 In a 9 × 13-inch ovenproof baking dish, arrange the sliced potatoes in an even layer. Top with some of the bacon mixture and season with a pinch each of salt and pepper. Continue to arrange the layers, as you would with a lasagna, seasoning each layer as you go.

7 Once you've used up all the ingredients, pour the cream overtop, then place the wedges of Reblochon on top of the tartiflette.

8 Bake in the oven for 25 minutes, or until the potatoes are cooked through. Let rest for about 5 minutes before serving.

NOTE: Reblochon can be tough to find sometimes. If you're having trouble, you can use Chaumes, Coulommiers, or Brie de Meaux instead. They're all French and have comparable flavor profiles to Reblochon.

Simple Vegetarian Pasta

PREP TIME: 10 MINUTES **COOK TIME:** 18 MINUTES **SERVES:** 4

1 lb (450 g) penne

3 Tbsp extra virgin olive oil

1 green onion, thinly chopped

1–2 tsp red pepper flakes, to taste

4 stalks asparagus, sliced into ½-inch pieces

2 large heirloom tomatoes, cut into wedges (see note)

3½ oz (100 g) Parmigiano-Reggiano, grated, divided

2½ oz (70 g) pecorino romano, grated, divided

Kosher salt

Freshly ground black pepper

Some years back, I was asked to create a pasta dish inspired by the farmers' market for *The Marilyn Denis Show*. This was a perfect pairing for me, because I love channeling my European roots and relying on the best ingredients that the season has to offer—and there's nowhere better than a farmers' market to find them. This result is super easy to make, yet delivers a lot of flavor in the fresh vegetables and salty cheeses. Depending on what's in season where you live, you can swap the asparagus for another quick-cooking vegetable.

1 Bring a large pot of salted water to a boil over medium-high heat.

2 Cook the pasta for 1 minute less than the cooking time written on the package. Just before it's finished cooking, carefully use a liquid measuring cup to reserve ½ cup of the cooking water. Drain the pasta into a colander.

3 In a large nonstick sauté pan on medium heat, cook the olive oil, green onions, and red pepper flakes for 2 minutes, stirring occasionally. Add the asparagus and tomatoes and continue to cook for 2 more minutes, stirring gently to incorporate the ingredients without mashing the tomatoes.

4 Add half of the pasta, a splash of the reserved cooking water, and half the amounts of both cheeses. Stir to bring together. Let the sauce reduce for 3–4 minutes, until the texture has thickened slightly.

5 Add the remaining pasta to the skillet and stir to combine. If you need more sauce, add a splash more of the cooking water and let it cook until thick. Once you're happy with the consistency, add the remaining cheeses and season with salt and pepper. Serve immediately.

NOTE: Don't make this dish in the wintertime! The tomatoes absolutely have to be in season, otherwise the dish will be flavorless and as depressing as an underripe winter tomato.

Halloumi Salad with Fresh Peas & Radishes

PREP TIME: 10 MINUTES **COOK TIME:** 3 MINUTES **SERVES:** 2

FOR THE VINAIGRETTE:

2½ Tbsp extra virgin olive oil

2 Tbsp champagne vinegar

Kosher salt

Freshly ground black pepper

¼ cup roughly chopped pistachios

¼ cup finely chopped fresh mint

2 Tbsp finely chopped fresh chives

FOR THE SALAD:

1 tsp extra virgin olive oil

7 oz (200 g) halloumi, cut into ¾-inch-thick pieces

5 radishes, quartered

½ cup fresh peas, blanched

1 package (5 oz) baby arugula

Crusty bread, for serving

Easter was always a huge thing in my house growing up. We'd celebrate with a beautiful lamb meal, with tons of side dishes that highlighted local spring vegetables. This salad would be a delicious accompaniment for a celebratory springtime dinner, but it's equally suitable as a light main on its own.

1 To make the vinaigrette, in a medium mixing bowl, whisk the olive oil, champagne vinegar, and a few pinches each of salt and pepper. Add the pistachios, mint, and chives to the mixing bowl and stir gently to combine. Set aside.

2 To make the salad, in a large nonstick skillet on high heat, add the olive oil to coat the surface of the pan. Place the halloumi slices in the pan and cook on both sides for about 1½ minutes on each side, until golden brown. Turn off the heat and set the pan aside.

3 In a medium mixing bowl, toss the radishes, peas, and arugula, without any dressing.

4 To serve, place the slices of halloumi on a large plate, running down the middle. Scatter the vegetables around them. Give the vinaigrette a quick whisk, then dress the vegetables well and serve the salad immediately with crusty bread on the side.

5-Cheese Mac & Cheese

PREP TIME: 20 MINUTES **COOK TIME:** 40 MINUTES **SERVES:** 4–6

- 1 cup shredded 3- to 5-year aged Ontario cheddar
- 1 cup shredded 1-year aged Dutch gouda
- ½ cup shredded Parmigiano-Reggiano
- ½ cup shredded Swiss gruyère
- ¼ cup shredded truffle-infused cheese (see note)
- 1 lb (450 g) macaroni or tubetti pasta
- ⅓ cup salted butter
- ¼ cup all-purpose flour
- 2½ cups whole milk
- A few pinches smoked paprika
- A few pinches grated fresh nutmeg
- Sea salt and freshly ground black pepper
- ½ cup panko breadcrumbs
- 1 Tbsp extra virgin olive oil
- 1 sprig fresh rosemary, leaves picked, for garnish

I can't be certain, but I believe I've been asked about 1 million times in my career what cheeses make the best mac and cheese. The problem is that my answer keeps changing—so many styles of cheese work and melt perfectly in a mac and cheese. For the purposes of this book, I couldn't choose just one representative, so we're doing a global version of mac and cheese with five different cheeses from around the world. Go big or go home!

1 Preheat the oven to 350°F and butter a large casserole dish.

2 Mix all the cheese in a large bowl, making sure to incorporate them together.

3 Bring a large pot of salted water to a boil over medium-high heat. Cook the pasta for 1 minute less than the package directions advise, then drain the water.

4 Heat a large saucepan over medium heat, then melt the butter. Sprinkle in the flour and whisk constantly until the mixture is smooth and combined. Add the milk slowly, whisking constantly to make a roux.

5 Reduce the heat to low and slowly add the shredded cheese blend a little at a time, whisking to melt and combine. Continue until you've added all the cheeses and you have a creamy, thick sauce.

6 Just before the sauce is done, add the paprika, nutmeg, and salt and pepper to taste.

7 Transfer the cooked pasta to the buttered casserole dish, then pour in the cheese sauce. Gently stir to combine.

8 Sprinkle the panko breadcrumbs overtop and drizzle with the olive oil.

9 Bake in the oven for 25–30 minutes, or until the top is golden brown and the sauce is bubbling. Let cool for a few minutes, then top with a few fresh rosemary leaves, and enjoy.

NOTE: A truffle-infused cheese is typically a pecorino or a gouda, but buy whatever you like best.

2019
MALBEC
CAHORS

Romantic Date Night Fondue for Two

PREP TIME: 20 MINUTES **COOK TIME:** 10 MINUTES **SERVES:** 2

FOR THE FONDUE:

5 oz (140 g) aged Swiss gruyère, shredded

5 oz (140 g) white English cheddar, shredded

5 oz (140 g) 6-month aged Dutch gouda, shredded

5 oz (140 g) Swiss Appenzeller, shredded

2 Tbsp cornstarch or all-purpose flour

1 clove garlic, halved

1 cup white wine

1 Tbsp fresh lemon juice

1 tsp grated fresh nutmeg

1 tsp freshly ground black pepper

1 tsp smoked paprika

FOR DIPPING:

Crusty baguette slices

8–10 boiled mini potatoes

1 bell pepper, thickly sliced

1 cured French sausage, sliced (I like rosette de Lyon)

1 crisp apple, sliced

1 bottle red wine

There is nothing better than a cold winter night, cozy pajamas, this fondue recipe, your loving partner, a bottle of good French red wine, and your favorite rom com—any Sandra Bullock fans here? This one goes out to all you hopeless romantics.

1 To make the fondue, in a large bowl, combine the gruyère, cheddar, gouda, and Appenzeller. Add the cornstarch, toss to coat the cheese, then set aside.

2 Rub the inside of a fondue pot or a medium pot with the halved garlic clove, then set over medium-high heat. Discard the garlic. Add the white wine and lemon juice and bring to a simmer.

3 Gradually add the shredded cheese blend, stirring slowly but constantly, until it's all in the pot and has reached a smooth, thick consistency, about 10 minutes.

4 Add the nutmeg, pepper, and paprika. Serve immediately with all your beautiful dipping accompaniments.

Niagara-Inspired Stromboli

PREP TIME: 20 MINUTES **COOK TIME:** 25 MINUTES **SERVES:** 2

Olive oil

1 ball (1 lb/450 g) store-bought pizza dough, room temperature

3 pieces jarred pepperoncini spicy peppers

3 pieces jarred roasted red peppers

⅓–½ cup crushed San Marzano tomatoes

10 slices mozzarella

10 slices hot soppressata

1 tsp dried oregano

1 tsp red pepper flakes

1 large egg

1 Tbsp grated Parmigiano-Reggiano

When my wife, Courtney, first made me a stromboli, I immediately fell in love with it. However, she also tried to convince me that this was an authentically Italian-inspired dish. And as much as I adored this dish, and as much as I love Courtney, no amount of convincing was going to sway me—this delicious cross between a pizza and calzone definitely doesn't come from Italy. We went back and forth for a while, until Courtney finally named this the Niagara-Inspired Stromboli, after the big Italian community in Port Colborne, Ontario, where she and her family are from. Italian or not, this recipe rocks and will be something you crave on a weekly basis.

1 Preheat the oven to 375°F and generously grease a 13 × 18-inch baking sheet with olive oil.

2 Place your pizza dough in a greased bowl on the counter to come to room temperature, if it isn't already.

3 Stretch the dough on the baking sheet into a rectangular shape. It should be able to stretch to the edges of the pan. If the dough isn't stretching easily, let it rest at room temperature for a bit longer and come back to it later.

4 Thinly slice the pepperoncini and roasted red peppers and set aside.

5 Once the dough is stretched evenly, spoon the crushed tomatoes overtop, using more if needed to evenly coat the entire surface.

6 Add the mozzarella slices in an even layer, covering the entire surface, followed by the soppressata. Sprinkle with oregano and red pepper flakes and distribute the roasted red peppers and pepperoncini spicy peppers evenly overtop.

7 Now it's time to roll! Starting with the long edge closest to you, roll your dough into a log shape as evenly as possible. This is essentially a rolled pizza. As you continue to roll it up, tuck the ends in to prevent spillage when baking.

8 Whisk the egg, then brush it all over the rolled stromboli. Sprinkle with the grated Parmigiano-Reggiano, then bake for 20–25 minutes, until the stromboli is golden brown. Let rest for 5 minutes before serving.

Modesta's Pasta e Ceci

PREP TIME: 5 MINUTES **COOK TIME:** 25 MINUTES **SERVES:** 4

6 oz (170 g) tubetti pasta

¼ cup extra virgin olive oil

4 cloves garlic, lightly crushed

2 sprigs fresh rosemary

Kosher salt

Freshly ground black pepper

½ tsp red pepper flakes

2 Tbsp tomato paste

3 Roma tomatoes, chopped

1 cup chicken or vegetable stock

2 cans (each 15 oz) chickpeas, drained and rinsed

3½ oz (100 g) Parmigiano-Reggiano, grated, divided

3½ oz (100 g) pecorino romano, grated, divided

Modesta Pristine is my incredible, loving, and selfless mother. She also happens to be one of the best cooks I know and was essentially the person who got me excited about cooking when I was a young child. My mom was born and raised in Avellino, a small town outside Naples in southern Italy. This area of the country is known for its rustic, simple, and delicious food, like this dish. It seems like just yesterday that my three brothers and I were enjoying this with a glass of milk at our dining room table. This one's for you, mom.

1 Bring a large pot of salted water to a boil over medium-high heat. Cook the tubetti for 1 minute less than the package directions advise, then drain and set aside.

2 In a large skillet over medium heat, heat the olive oil. Add the garlic, rosemary sprigs, and a pinch each of salt and pepper. Cook for a few minutes, until the garlic softens.

3 Add the red pepper flakes, tomato paste, and tomatoes. Cook for 3–4 minutes, until the tomatoes are soft and have released their liquid, then remove and discard the rosemary sprigs.

4 Pour in the stock and chickpeas and let the sauce reduce for about 5 minutes, until thickened.

5 Add the cooked pasta and stir to combine. Add about three-quarters of both the Parmigiano-Reggiano and pecorino romano cheeses, and stir to incorporate. Remove the skillet from the heat.

6 Divide the pasta among 4 plates, garnish with the remaining cheeses, and serve.

Kim Family Cheese Dakgalbi

PREP TIME: 15 MINUTES + MARINATING **COOK TIME:** 16 MINUTES **SERVES:** 4–6

FOR THE MARINATED TOFU:

1 block (14–16 oz/400–450 g) firm tofu

2 Tbsp soy sauce

1 Tbsp gochujang

1 Tbsp gochugaru or red pepper flakes

1 Tbsp mirin or white cooking wine

1 Tbsp sesame oil

1 Tbsp brown sugar

2 cloves garlic, minced

1 small onion, thinly sliced

FOR THE STIR-FRY:

1 Tbsp vegetable oil

1 sweet potato, peeled and thinly sliced

1 cup shredded green cabbage

1 cup shredded carrots

1 cup sliced green bell peppers

1 cup sliced green zucchini

2 green onions, cut into 2-inch pieces

1 cup grated high-moisture mozzarella

2–3 cups steamed white rice, for serving (optional)

This is an amazing recipe inspired by my close friend Jennifer Kim. Jennifer and my wife, Courtney, went to university together many years ago. They have been besties since then, but the friendship reached new levels when we all became roommates for a year. Since then, Jenn has become a sister to me, and like any great family member, she taught me the recipes she'd grown up eating. Jenn's parents were born and raised in South Korea. I was so grateful to learn about Korean food culture from the Kim family (and I always looked forward to the leftovers Mrs. Kim would send home with Jenn), and this recipe is one of my all-time favorites. It's simple, cheesy, and incredibly satisfying.

1 To make the marinated tofu, start by wrapping the tofu in paper towel and placing a cast-iron skillet or heavy-bottomed pot on top. This will press out the liquid.

2 Meanwhile, make the marinade. In a large bowl, combine the soy sauce, gochujang, gochugaru, mirin, sesame oil, brown sugar, garlic, and onions. Set aside.

3 Unwrap the tofu and cut into bite-sized cubes. Add the tofu cubes to the marinade, making sure each piece is well coated. Cover the bowl with plastic wrap and let it marinate for at least 30 minutes or up to 1 hour.

4 To make the stir-fry, heat a large nonstick skillet or a wok over medium-high heat. Add the vegetable oil.

5 Once the oil is just starting to smoke, add the marinated tofu to the skillet and stir-fry until the tofu is slightly caramelized, 5–7 minutes. Don't stir it too vigorously—you want to let it brown without breaking.

6 Add the sweet potatoes, cabbage, carrots, bell peppers, and zucchini. Stir-fry for another 5–7 minutes, until the vegetables are tender. If the mixture seems too dry, you can add a splash of water to create a bit of a sauce.

7 Once the tofu and vegetables are cooked, sprinkle the green onions overtop and cover the whole stir-fry with grated mozzarella.

8 Reduce the heat to low, cover the skillet with a lid, and let the cheese melt for about 2 minutes, or until it becomes ooey-gooey and deliciously creamy.

9 Serve the stir-fry immediately with a side of steamed white rice or on its own.

Superstar Greek Pastitsio

PREP TIME: 15 MINUTES **COOK TIME:** 1 HOUR, 25 MINUTES **SERVES:** 4 + LEFTOVERS

FOR THE PASTA:

1 lb (450 g) bucatini pasta

2 Tbsp extra virgin olive oil

1 Tbsp salted butter

¼ cup grated kefalotyri or myzithra cheese

Kosher salt

FOR THE MEAT SAUCE:

1 Tbsp extra virgin olive oil

1 cooking onion, finely chopped

2 cloves garlic, minced

1 lb (450 g) ground beef

1 can (14 oz) crushed tomatoes

2 Tbsp tomato paste

1 tsp dried Greek oregano

½ tsp ground cinnamon

Kosher salt

Freshly ground black pepper

FOR THE BÉCHAMEL SAUCE:

¼ cup salted butter

¼ cup all-purpose flour

2 cups whole milk

1 cup grated kefalotyri or myzithra cheese

Kosher salt

1 pinch ground nutmeg

2 large eggs

When I was filming my show in Athens a few years ago, I hosted superstar chef Akis Petretzikis as a guest. Chef Akis is easily the most influential Greek chef in the world today, and he taught me a lot about Greek food. This recipe, which is almost like a Greek version of lasagna, is my ode to Chef Akis, but it also happens to be my "stuck on a desert island" dish—if it was the last thing I ever ate, I wouldn't be disappointed.

1 To make the pasta, bring a large pot of salted water to a boil over high heat. Cook the pasta for 1 minute less than the package directions advise. Drain the pasta, return it to the pot, and toss with the olive oil, butter, grated kefalotyri cheese, and a pinch of salt. Set aside.

2 To make the meat sauce, in a large saucepan, heat the olive oil over medium heat. Add the chopped onions and garlic and sauté until the onions are translucent, about 3 minutes. Add the beef and cook until browned, about 5 minutes, breaking it up with a wooden spoon. If there is over ½ cup of fat in the pan, drain it with a ladle. Stir in the crushed tomatoes, tomato paste, oregano, cinnamon, salt, and pepper. Simmer the sauce for 15 minutes, or until it thickens. Set aside.

3 To make the béchamel sauce, in a separate saucepan over medium heat, melt the butter. Stir in the flour and cook for 1–2 minutes, until it forms a paste.

4 Gradually whisk in the milk, making sure there are no lumps, and continue stirring until the sauce thickens and coats the back of a spoon, 5–7 minutes. Remove the saucepan from the heat and stir in the grated kefalotyri cheese, salt, and nutmeg.

5 Preheat the oven to 350°F and lightly grease a 9 × 13-inch baking dish with olive oil.

6 In a mixing bowl, lightly beat the eggs, then slowly add a ladle of the béchamel sauce, whisking constantly, to temper them. Once the eggs are warmed, slowly add the egg mixture to the béchamel sauce, stirring constantly to incorporate.

7 To assemble the pastitsio, spread half of the cooked pasta in the prepared baking dish. Add all the meat sauce, spreading it out evenly to cover. Place the remaining pasta overtop the meat sauce, then pour the béchamel overtop, spreading it evenly.

8 Bake the pastitsio in the oven for 40–45 minutes, or until the top is golden and bubbling. Remove from the oven and let it rest for 10 minutes before serving.

Jam Rock Jerk Macaroni Pie

PREP TIME: 12 MINUTES **COOK TIME:** 50 MINUTES **SERVES:** 4

FOR THE MAC AND CHEESE:

½ lb (225 g) elbow macaroni

2 Tbsp unsalted butter

1 Tbsp all-purpose flour

1 cup whole milk

2 cups grated 5-year aged cheddar, divided

Kosher salt

Freshly ground black pepper

FOR THE JERK SEASONING:

2 tsp ground allspice

1 tsp ground thyme

1 tsp smoked paprika

1 tsp garlic powder

1 tsp onion powder

½ tsp cayenne pepper

½ tsp ground nutmeg

½ tsp brown sugar

Kosher salt

Freshly ground black pepper

FOR THE TOPPING:

1 cup breadcrumbs

2 Tbsp melted unsalted butter

I haven't taken many vacations over my career, but when I do, I love going to Jamaica, and macaroni pie is one of my favorite things to eat while I'm there. It's a staple of Jamaican cuisine, and I was so grateful to learn a recipe for it from a friend and colleague, Latoya Fagan. Latoya is a powerhouse of a chef. She has cooked for the Toronto Raptors, and she owns her own catering company, which highlights the traditional Jamaican and Caribbean dishes from her youth.

1 To make the mac and cheese, bring a large pot of salted water to a boil over high heat. Cook the elbow macaroni for 1 minute less than the package directions advise. Drain the pasta and set aside.

2 Preheat the oven to 350°F and grease an 8-inch square baking dish with olive oil.

3 In a large saucepan over medium heat, melt the butter. Stir in the flour and cook for 1–2 minutes, until it forms a paste. Gradually whisk in the milk, stirring constantly to avoid lumps. Continue stirring until the mixture thickens and coats the back of a spoon, 5–7 minutes.

4 Add about three-quarters of the grated cheddar to the sauce, reserving a small amount for the topping. Stir until the cheese melts and the sauce is creamy. Season with salt and pepper to taste.

5 To make the jerk seasoning, in a small bowl, mix all the seasoning ingredients, and a pinch each of salt and pepper.

6 Add 1 tablespoon of the jerk seasoning to the cheese sauce, mixing well to incorporate the flavors. Stir the cooked pasta into the cheese sauce, ensuring that all the pasta is evenly coated, then pour the whole thing into the prepared baking dish.

7 To make the topping, in a separate bowl, mix the breadcrumbs, melted butter, and 1 tablespoon of jerk seasoning until well combined. Sprinkle the breadcrumb mixture and the reserved grated cheddar over the pasta.

8 Bake the jerk macaroni pie in the preheated oven for 25–30 minutes, or until the top is golden and the edges are bubbling. Remove the macaroni pie from the oven and let it cool slightly before serving.

TIAGO'S PORTUGUESE POTATOES
(p. 124)

Arruda Family Portuguese Chicken

PREP TIME: 35 MINUTES + MARINATING **COOK TIME:** 1 HOUR **SERVES:** 4–6

- 4–6 piri piri peppers (also called bird's eye chilies)
- 4 cloves garlic
- 1 tsp smoked paprika
- 1 tsp dried oregano
- 1 tsp ground cumin
- ¼ cup fresh lemon juice
- ¼ cup extra virgin olive oil
- Kosher salt
- Freshly ground black pepper
- One 3–4 lb (1.4–1.8 kg) chicken, cleaned and patted dry (see note)
- Lemon wedges, for garnish
- Fresh oregano leaves, for garnish

My sister-in-law Melissa is of Portuguese descent. I have never been to Portugal and I didn't grow up eating Portuguese food, but I've grown to absolutely love it. It was always a treat to visit my youngest brother Arian and Melissa's house, as that's where I would satiate my Portuguese food craving. It was extra special when Melissa's parents were over, because her mom would often make this chicken recipe. Now it's something I make on my own every few weeks. You'll notice that there's no cheese in this recipe, but don't be alarmed—it's meant to be served with Tiago's Portuguese Potatoes (p. 124), which features São Jorge, a gorgeous Portuguese cheese.

1 In a food processor or blender, combine the piri piri peppers, garlic, paprika, oregano, cumin, lemon juice, olive oil, and a few pinches of salt and pepper. Blend until smooth, taste, and adjust the seasoning, if needed.

2 Place the chicken in a large bowl and pour the marinade overtop, making sure the chicken is well coated on all sides and in every joint. Cover the bowl and refrigerate for 2–4 hours—the longer, the better.

3 Remove the marinated chicken from the fridge and let it come to room temperature for about 30 minutes. In the meantime, preheat the oven to 400°F.

4 Place the chicken on a roasting pan or baking sheet and bake for about 1 hour, or until the internal temperature reaches 165°F. Once cooked, remove from the oven and let the chicken rest for at least 10 minutes before carving it into pieces.

5 Place the chicken pieces on a large serving platter and pour the pan drippings overtop—there's tons of flavor there. Garnish with lemon wedges and fresh oregano leaves, and enjoy.

NOTE: If you like, you can ask your butcher to cut the chicken into pieces before you cook it, but you'll need to adjust your cooking time accordingly.

Tiago's Portuguese Potatoes

PREP TIME: 15 MINUTES **COOK TIME:** 40 MINUTES **SERVES:** 4

This is a special recipe that Cheese Boutique's executive chef Tiago Milheiro and I came up with. Tiago was born and raised in Portugal. He's been our chef for many years, and I've learned so much about Portuguese cuisine from him. I asked him years ago for a fun poutine dish that we could cook from our food truck for a special event. He mentioned a classic Portuguese potato dish that's similar to poutine, and this is what he made. These potatoes are paired with the Arruda Family Portuguese Chicken in the image on page 122—make both for a fantastic dinner.

FOR THE POTATOES:

4 large Yukon Gold potatoes

Grapeseed oil, for frying

Kosher salt

FOR THE SAUCE:

¼ cup extra virgin olive oil (Tiago says Portuguese oil is a must!)

1 small onion, finely chopped

Kosher salt

2 cloves garlic, minced

1 tsp smoked paprika

½ tsp cayenne pepper

½ tsp ground cumin

½ cup crushed tomatoes

½ tsp sugar

½ tsp red pepper flakes

Freshly ground black pepper

FOR SERVING:

3½ oz (100 g) São Jorge cheese, coarsely grated (see note)

2 Tbsp chopped fresh flatleaf parsley, for garnish

NOTE: If you can't find São Jorge cheese, substitute with a Spanish manchego.

1 To make the potatoes, peel the potatoes and cut into bite-sized cubes. Bring a large pot of salted water to a boil, then cook the potatoes for about 8 minutes, until a fork can pierce through them easily but they still hold their shape. Drain the potatoes and set aside.

2 In a large, deep skillet over high heat, heat about 2 inches of grapeseed oil to 350°F. To check if the oil is hot enough, place the handle of a wooden spoon in the oil—if bubbles form around the handle, the oil is ready.

3 Working in batches so as not to overcrowd the pan, fry the potatoes for 5–7 minutes, flipping them halfway through, until golden brown and crispy on all sides. With a slotted spoon, transfer the fried potatoes to a baking sheet lined with paper towel to drain any excess oil. Sprinkle the potatoes with salt while they're still hot. Continue until all the potatoes are fried.

4 While the potatoes are frying, make the sauce. In a medium saucepan over medium heat, heat the olive oil. Add the chopped onions and a pinch of salt and cook until the onions are soft and translucent.

5 Add the garlic, paprika, cayenne, and cumin. Cook for 1 minute, stirring constantly, until you really smell the spices and garlic, then add the crushed tomatoes, sugar, red pepper flakes, and salt and pepper to taste.

6 Simmer the sauce for 10–15 minutes, allowing the flavors to meld and the sauce to thicken. Once the sauce is fairly smooth, remove it from the heat and adjust the seasoning, if needed.

7 To serve, arrange the crispy fried potatoes on a serving dish, drizzle the sauce over the potatoes, and add the grated São Jorge cheese overtop. The warmth of the potatoes and sauce will soften the cheese. Let the dish sit for 1–2 minutes, then garnish with parsley and dig in.

CHEESE SPOTLIGHT: SÃO JORGE

#13 in Afrim's Top 13 Hidden-Gem Cheeses (p. 30)

Duck Confit Poutine

PREP TIME: 15 MINUTES + SOAKING **COOK TIME:** 40 MINUTES **SERVES:** 2

2 precooked duck confit legs (see note)

5 oz (140 g) cheese curds

FOR THE FRIES:

4 large russet potatoes

Vegetable or grapeseed oil, for frying

Kosher salt

FOR THE GRAVY:

¼ cup salted butter

¼ cup all-purpose flour

2 cups beef stock

2 tsp Worcestershire sauce

Kosher salt

Freshly ground black pepper

4 lemon wedges, for serving (optional)

NOTE: You can buy pre-cooked duck confit legs at a butcher shop or high-end food store. They typically come vacuum-packed.

This recipe is a Canadian classic and hits the spot on a cold, wet day. Put on your comfiest pjs, open a cold bottle of lager, throw on some Shania Twain, and make this together with your loved one. It takes a bit of time, but the richness of the roasted duck and the savory poutine is worth it.

1 Preheat the oven to 375°F and remove the duck confit legs from the packaging. Place in a baking dish, skin side up, and roast for 20 minutes, or until crispy and golden brown. Let cool, then shred the meat from the bones.

2 While the duck cooks, make the fries. Peel the potatoes and cut them into long, ½-inch-thick strips. Place the potatoes in a large bowl of cold water for 30 minutes to remove some of the starch. After they've soaked, transfer the potatoes to a clean dish towel and dry them very well.

3 In a large Dutch oven over medium-high heat, heat 3–4 inches of oil, enough to submerge the potatoes. The oil temperature should reach 350°F. To test if it's hot enough, place the handle of a wooden spoon in the oil. If bubbles form around the handle, the oil is ready.

4 Working in batches so as not to overcrowd the pot, use a slotted spoon to gently lower the potatoes into the hot oil. Fry the potatoes for 3–4 minutes. They won't yet be golden. Remove the potatoes, again using a slotted spoon, and let them drain on a baking sheet lined with paper towel. Return them to the hot oil to cook for an additional 2–3 minutes, until perfectly golden brown. Transfer them back to the paper towel to drain, and sprinkle with salt while still hot. Repeat with the remaining potatoes.

5 If you can manage the timing (or your partner is in the kitchen and can help!), make the gravy while you cook the fries so that everything comes together at the same time. In a saucepan over medium heat, melt the butter. Add the flour and whisk constantly for 2–3 minutes, until a smooth paste forms. Gradually pour in the beef stock, whisking constantly to prevent lumps. Continue whisking until the gravy is smooth and thick. Add the Worcestershire and season with salt and pepper. If the gravy becomes too thick, thin it out by adding a bit more stock or water. Once you're happy with it, remove the gravy from the heat.

6 To assemble the dish, place the fries on a large plate. Add the shredded duck confit and cheese curds, then drizzle a healthy amount of hot gravy overtop. Don't overdo it on the gravy, but don't be stingy with it either. Squeeze over lemon juice, if you like, and enjoy immediately.

Raclette Supernova

PREP TIME: 20 MINUTES **COOK TIME:** 3 MINUTES **SERVES:** 4

ACCOMPANIMENTS:

2–3 links landjäger sausage or high-quality beef jerky, sliced

7 oz (200 g) bündnerfleisch or another smoked and cured beef, sliced

7 oz (200 g) rosette de Lyon sausage or another dried pork sausage, sliced

1 lb mini potatoes, boiled and cooled

1 Honeycrisp apple, sliced

1 crusty French baguette, sliced

1 head broccoli, cut into florets

1 small jar cornichons

12–14 oz (340–400 g) raclette, sliced ¼ inch thick (ask your cheesemonger to slice it for you; see note)

Freshly ground black pepper

There are some winter days, when it's cold and snowing outside, that Courtney will call me at the store and ask, "Is it a raclette kind of night?" My answer is always yes. Setting up a raclette dinner is easy and fun, but it also feels special. This is a recipe you need to plan for in advance, as you do need some specialized equipment, but you can source a raclette grill easily online, and then you too can call your partner on a random Tuesday and ask for a raclette night!

1 Make sure all your accompaniments are prepped and ready to eat.

2 Turn on your raclette grill to heat, then put a slice or two of raclette cheese on the small plates that come with your grill and sit underneath the heating element. Let the cheese melt for 30–45 seconds—that's all it takes!

3 Scrape the cheese on an accompaniment of your choosing, and garnish with freshly ground black pepper, if you like. Keep repeating until the raclette has defeated you. Here's my ultimate bite: baguette, topped with potato, raclette spread on top, and garnished with a cornichon and black pepper. I call this a Raclette Supernova.

NOTE: I'm approximating 3–3½ oz (85–100 g) of raclette per person for this recipe, but feel free to scale up or down as you like.

Gnocchi al Pomodoro

PREP TIME: 10 MINUTES **COOK TIME:** 18 MINUTES **SERVES:** 2

10 oz (280 g) gnocchi

Extra virgin olive oil

½ yellow onion, finely diced

2 cloves garlic, finely chopped

2 tsp red pepper flakes

7 oz (200 g) pancetta, cubed

¼ can (7 oz) San Marzano tomatoes (about ¾ cup)

4 tsp heavy cream

2½ oz (70 g) Parmigiano-Reggiano, grated, divided

2½ oz (70 g) pecorino romano, grated, divided

Kosher salt

Freshly ground black pepper

2 Tbsp fresh flatleaf parsley, for garnish

2–4 slices hearty bread, for serving

Here I'm busting out my Neapolitan roots with a recipe I created for World Pasta Day a few years ago. It brings together southern Italian flavors, top-quality products, and lots of love. Buy the best you can afford for this one, as it makes a big difference to the result. I grew up eating dishes like this—I hope you approve, Mom.

1 Bring a large pot of salted water to a boil over high heat. Cook the gnocchi for about 3 minutes, or until the gnocchi float to the top. Drain the gnocchi, drizzle with a touch of olive oil so that they don't stick together, and set aside.

2 Meanwhile, in a large nonstick skillet over medium heat, warm 1 tablespoon of olive oil.

3 Add the onions, garlic, and red pepper flakes and sauté for about 3 minutes, until the onions are soft and translucent. Add the pancetta and cook for another 4 minutes, or until the fat renders out.

4 Gently stir in the tomatoes and break them up slightly with a wooden spoon. You want to maintain some texture in the tomatoes, so you don't need to break them up too much. Cook for another 4–5 minutes, or until the sauce starts to reduce.

5 Pour in the cream, stirring constantly for 2–3 minutes to create a creamy texture. Add about three-quarters of both cheeses and stir until melted. At this point, add a few pinches of salt and pepper, taste, and adjust the seasoning as needed.

6 Once you're happy with the sauce, gently add the cooked gnocchi and toss until coated.

7 Transfer to a serving dish, garnish with parsley, and sprinkle the remaining cheese overtop. Enjoy immediately and soak up any extra sauce with the bread, like a true southern Italian!

NOTE: The Parmigiano-Reggiano adds a sharp nuttiness to the dish and the pecorino romano adds a nice saltiness. You need both cheeses for that full umami flavor.

Cheese Boutique Insiders' Saag Paneer

PREP TIME: 30 MINUTES **COOK TIME:** 35 MINUTES **SERVES:** 4–6

4 Tbsp vegetable oil, divided

8 oz (225 g) paneer, cut into 1-inch cubes

1 red onion, roughly chopped

4 cloves garlic

1 serrano chili pepper, seeds removed for less heat

1 jar (24 oz) tomato passata

1 Tbsp ground coriander

1 Tbsp ground cumin

½ tsp cayenne pepper

¼ tsp ground turmeric

Kosher salt

1 lb baby spinach, roughly chopped

½ cup water

½ cup heavy cream

½ tsp garam masala

½ lemon

Steamed white rice, for serving

Being of Mediterranean descent, I didn't grow up eating Indian or South Asian–inspired food, but once I started working alongside some of the Indian chefs at Cheese Boutique, I fell in love with the flavors. I now crave certain Indian dishes all the time. We've had quite a few Indian chefs in our kitchens at the store over the years, and they taught me this dish. It's an oldie of a recipe, but it's a goody.

1 In a large nonstick skillet over medium heat, heat 2 tablespoons of vegetable oil for about 2 minutes.

2 Add the paneer and cook for about 2 minutes, until browned on the underside, then flip and cook for another 2 minutes. Transfer the paneer to a bowl and cover with a warm, damp cloth to keep it warm and soft.

3 In a food processor, pulse the onions, garlic, and serrano chili until minced. Add a tablespoon or two of water to help it become a paste.

4 In a large saucepan over medium heat, heat the remaining 2 tablespoons oil until it shimmers. Add the onion paste and cook until light brown and some of it sticks to the bottom of the pan, about 2 minutes. Stir in the tomato passata, coriander, cumin, cayenne, turmeric, and a healthy pinch of salt. Turn the heat down to low and simmer, partially covered, for about 10 minutes.

5 Add the spinach and cook, covered, for about 4 minutes, until the spinach has wilted. Stir in the ½ cup water and simmer, covered, until the spinach turns a dark green, about 15 minutes.

6 Add the paneer, cream, and garam masala. Continue to simmer the curry, covered but stirring occasionally, for 5 minutes to let the flavors come together. Squeeze in some lemon juice, and stir to incorporate. Serve with steamed white rice.

CHEESE SPOTLIGHT: MAHÓN

#7 in Afrim's Top 13 Hidden-Gem Cheeses (p. 30)

Dessert

Certain cheeses are specifically made as a sweet after-dinner treat. Can you imagine how pathetic a tiramisu would be without mascarpone? Here are some gorgeous recipes to end your evening with a smile.

Poached Rhubarb & Goat Cheese

PREP TIME: 5 MINUTES **COOK TIME:** 8 MINUTES **SERVES:** 2

2½ Tbsp water

2 Tbsp honey

1 pinch freshly ground black pepper

2 stalks rhubarb, sliced ½ inch thick

Zest of ⅓ orange

½ tsp vanilla extract

1 package (3½ oz/100 g) goat cheese

2 Tbsp finely chopped fresh mint

1 pinch kosher salt

4–6 shortbread cookies

I am not a pastry chef and I don't make desserts often, but when I do want to step outside my comfort zone, I rely on gorgeous, local ingredients whenever possible. Here, I'm pairing tart rhubarb with fresh, sour goat cheese. Both highlight the best that Ontario has to offer, so this dessert is a natural fit for me.

1 In a medium sauté pan over medium heat, combine the water, honey, and black pepper and cook for 2–3 minutes, until the mixture starts to thicken.

2 Add the rhubarb and cook down for 3 minutes, stirring occasionally.

3 Add the orange zest and vanilla. Gently stir and cook for about 2 minutes, or until the liquid has reduced and almost looks like a glaze. Remove the pan from the heat.

4 In a small mixing bowl, combine the goat cheese, mint, and salt. With a wooden spoon, stir vigorously.

5 Transfer the goat cheese to a plate and pour the glazed rhubarb overtop, along with any liquid in the pan. Serve with shortbread.

Aged Quebecois Cheddar Cookies

PREP TIME: 7 MINUTES **COOK TIME:** 15 MINUTES **MAKES:** 12–14 COOKIES

½ cup unsalted butter, room temperature

1½ cups grated 3- to 5-year aged Quebec cheddar

1 cup all-purpose flour

¼ tsp kosher salt

¼ tsp smoked paprika

¼ tsp freshly ground black pepper

½ cup finely chopped walnuts

1 large egg yolk

1 tsp cold water

I know this recipe may sound weird, but these savory and cheesy cookies will impress any guests. I first tasted them while traveling in Quebec many years ago, and they blew my mind. These cookies are a perfect addition to a charcuterie board, but they're equally wonderful served after dinner with a cup of tea. For this recipe, I'd recommend using a big, bold, rich cheddar from Quebec, which tends to be a bit more intense than its Ontario or even English counterparts. My ode to La Belle Province!

1 Preheat the oven to 350°F and line a baking sheet with parchment paper.

2 In a mixing bowl and using an electric handheld mixer or a sturdy whisk, cream the butter until smooth and lighter in color. Add the grated cheddar and mix until well combined.

3 In a separate bowl, whisk the flour, salt, paprika, and pepper.

4 Add the dry ingredients to the butter-cheese mixture. Mix until the dough starts coming together. Add the walnuts and mix until evenly distributed.

5 In a small bowl, beat the egg yolk with the cold water, and set aside.

6 Roll the dough into small balls, about 2 tablespoons each, and place them on the prepared baking sheet, about 1 inch apart. Flatten each ball slightly with the back of a fork.

7 Brush the tops of the cookies with the egg wash.

8 Bake for 12–15 minutes, or until cookies are golden brown around the edges. Let cool on the baking sheet before eating.

Stollen & Blue Cheese Holiday Dessert

PREP TIME: 2 MINUTES **COOK TIME:** 4 MINUTES **SERVES:** 4

- 1 stollen bread, filling of your choice
- 1 jar (6 oz) clotted cream
- 7 oz (200 g) Bleu d'Auvergne or another crumbly blue cheese
- One 3½ oz dark (60%) chocolate bar
- ¼ cup roughly chopped toasted hazelnuts

Stollen is a traditional German and Austrian Christmas bread filled with marzipan, candied fruit, and lots of butter—and notably for me, it pairs so well with cheese. I discovered this one wintry night in December over 10 years ago. I was creating a holiday cheese platter for friends and I needed to fill up the board with what I had at home. I had a stollen that I'd originally bought to give to a German neighbor, but my needs came first, and onto the cheese platter it went. The result was pure holiday magic.

1 Cut the stollen into finger-thick slices.

2 Heat a large nonstick skillet over medium heat. Toast the stollen for about 2 minutes on each side, until crispy and brown. There's no need to add any butter to the pan, as there's lots of butter in the bread already!

3 Place a dollop of clotted cream on the bread slices and smooth it out into an even layer.

4 Crumble some blue cheese on the layer of cream. Be fairly liberal here. It's the holidays, after all.

5 With a rasp or Microplane, grate the dark chocolate as finely as you can onto the blue cheese. Add a sprinkle of hazelnuts as a garnish. Repeat with the remaining slices of bread, and serve the slices on a large platter.

Tarte au Sucre avec Bleu d'Elizabeth

PREP TIME: 10 MINUTES + CHILLING **COOK TIME:** 40 MINUTES **MAKES:** ONE 9-INCH PIE

Adding blue cheese to a dessert is a surefire way into my heart. *Tarte au sucre*, which translates to "sugar pie," is another Quebecois classic. Here I'm combining sweetness with the saltiness of another classic Quebecois ingredient, Bleu d'Elizabeth. For me, this blue cheese sits in the top 5 worldwide. The cheese maker, Jean Morin, is a wonderful friend who has taught me so much.

FOR THE PIE CRUST:

1¼ cups all-purpose flour

½ tsp kosher salt

½ cup cold unsalted butter, cut into small cubes

¾ cup ice water

FOR THE FILLING:

1 cup brown sugar

¼ cup all-purpose flour

1 cup heavy cream

1 tsp vanilla extract

2 Tbsp unsalted butter, melted

3½ oz (100 g) Bleu d'Elizabeth or another blue cheese, crumbled and slightly chilled

1 To make the pie crust, in a food processor, pulse the flour and salt. Add the cold butter cubes and pulse until the mixture resembles coarse crumbs. Gradually add the ice water, 1 tablespoon at a time, and pulse until the dough holds together when pinched.

2 Turn the dough out onto a floured surface and gently knead it a few times to bring it together. Shape it into a round disk, wrap it in plastic wrap, and refrigerate for at least 1 hour.

3 When ready to bake, preheat the oven to 350°F.

4 Remove the chilled dough from the fridge, and roll it out to a circle about 11 inches in diameter—enough to fill a 9-inch pie plate. Carefully transfer the dough to the pie plate. Crimp the edges, trimming any excess overhanging pastry. Return the pie crust to the fridge for a few minutes to chill.

5 To make the filling, in a large bowl, whisk the brown sugar and flour. Gradually whisk in the cream until the mixture is smooth. Stir in the vanilla and melted butter.

6 Remove the pie crust from the fridge and pour in the filling. Bake for 30–40 minutes, until the filling is set and slightly caramelized on top.

7 Remove the pie from the oven and let it cool on a wire rack. While the pie is cooling, scatter the crumbled Bleu d'Elizabeth cheese evenly overtop. The warmth of the pie will soften the cheese.

Nostalgic Cannoli

PREP TIME: 30 MINUTES **MAKES:** 12 CANNOLI

1 tub (1 lb/450 g) mascarpone

1 lb (450 g) fresh ricotta (p. 88, or see note)

1 pinch kosher salt

1 pinch freshly ground black pepper

5 oz (140 g) crispy milk chocolate pearls

Zest of 1 lemon

1 Tbsp vanilla extract

1 tsp almond extract

½ cup roughly chopped pistachios

½ cup shaved dark (60%) chocolate

12 store-bought cannoli shells

A few years ago, I was the guest celebrity chef on a Royal Caribbean cruise around the Mediterranean, with stops in Mallorca, Rome, Naples, and Barcelona. It was awesome. I led cooking demos and cheese tastings for thousands of guests during the trip, and I led cooking classes in Rome and Naples. I called in a few favors from some chef friends, and we ended up learning to make pizza at the famous Neapolitan pizzeria La Gustosa. After the class, the twenty-five guests and I were on a pizza high, but even better, we were in the heart of my mom's hometown, where I spent many summer vacations with my family. As we wandered the streets, we stumbled on an incredible pastry shop, Antica Pasticceria, and suddenly I was a little boy again, walking hand in hand with my mom and gazing in awe at all the beautiful homemade Neapolitan pastries. I bought each guest a gelato, but I got myself a cannoli—my mom's favorite treat.

1 In a large mixing bowl, combine the mascarpone, ricotta, salt, and pepper. Use a wooden spoon, like Mama Pristine does. You're looking for a super-smooth, creamy consistency.

2 Add the milk chocolate pearls, lemon zest, and vanilla and almond extracts and incorporate well.

3 Fill a piping bag with the cheese mixture, or fill a large resealable plastic bag, pushing the mixture into one corner and then snipping off about 1 inch of the bottom corner edge. Set aside.

4 Scatter the pistachios on a small plate, and the dark chocolate shavings on another plate.

5 Slowly and gently, fill your cannoli shells. I like starting on one side halfway into the shell, then filling up the remaining half from the other opening. You want to slightly overfill them so your cheese mixture is creeping over the edges of both sides of the shell.

6 Gently press one end of the stuffed cannoli shell into the dark chocolate so it covers the exposed filling, and do the same on the other side with the pistachios. Enjoy immediately—cannoli are best when they're freshly stuffed.

NOTE: For the optimal cannoli, use the Homemade Ricotta recipe (p. 88), but if you are buying it commercially, find the freshest one you can.

My Turkish Family Künefe

PREP TIME: 15 MINUTES **COOK TIME:** 45 MINUTES **SERVES:** 8

- ½ lb (225 g) shredded phyllo dough
- ½ cup salted butter, melted
- 1½ Tbsp whole milk
- 4 oz (115 g) fresh bufala mozzarella, grated (see note)
- 12 oz (340 g) fresh ricotta (p. 88, or see note)
- ½ cup ground pistachios, 2 Tbsp reserved for garnish
- 2 Tbsp icing sugar
- ¼ tsp grated fresh nutmeg
- 3 cups water
- 1 cup white sugar
- ½ cup brown sugar
- 1 Tbsp fresh lemon juice
- 4 drops orange blossom water

My father, Fatos, was born in 1942, during the Second World War. He and his family left their home of Albania and went to Turkey to escape the war, and Turkey became their adopted home for much of my dad's adolescence. To this day, many of our family members still live there, and my parents have a summer home in Çeşme, a resort town on the Aegean Sea. Picture clear blue skies and a strong sense of culinary identity—fresh fish, simply treated produce, and lots of cheese-inspired desserts. It can be difficult to find Turkish cheese in North America, despite how fantastic and famous it is, so I've used cheeses that are easy to source for this classic Turkish dessert.

1 Preheat the oven to 375°F.

2 In a food processor, pulse the shredded phyllo dough to chop it finely. Add the butter and milk and pulse to combine.

3 Transfer half of the phyllo mixture to an 8-inch square baking dish, and press into the bottom and corners, making an even layer. Set the other half aside.

4 In a large bowl, mix the bufala mozzarella, ricotta, pistachios, icing sugar, and nutmeg.

5 Spread the cheese filling in an even layer on the shredded phyllo in the baking dish, then top with the remaining phyllo. Bake in the oven for 45 minutes.

6 While the pastry bakes, make a simple syrup. In a saucepan over high heat, bring the water to a boil, then add the white and brown sugars and the lemon juice. Cook until the syrup has reduced by about one-third and has a honey-like consistency. Remove the pot from the heat and stir in the orange blossom water.

7 Once the künefe is golden brown, remove it from the oven and set the pan on a wire rack to cool. Ladle two-thirds of the warm syrup gently overtop the künefe. To serve, cut into squares, garnish with a pinch of ground pistachios, and let guests add more syrup to their own individual pieces if they wish.

NOTE: For both the bufala mozzarella and the ricotta in this recipe, find the freshest options possible. You can even make your own ricotta with the recipe on p. 88.

Basque Cheesecake

PREP TIME: 15 MINUTES + COOLING **COOK TIME:** 45 MINUTES **SERVES:** 8–10

2.2 lb (1 kg) Philadelphia brick-style cream cheese, room temperature

2 cups sugar

1 tsp vanilla extract

1 pinch sea salt

7 large eggs, room temperature

2 cups heavy cream, room temperature

1 Tbsp all-purpose flour

I've had versions of this recipe a dozen different times while sitting on a bar stool in Barcelona or Madrid, or at Bar Raval in Toronto with my wife, and I've loved them all. Basque cheesecake doesn't have a lot of ingredients, so it's important to pick the right ones. Here, as strange as it sounds, the best cream cheese for the job is the industrially made one that you can find at every supermarket. Don't try to use a higher-end spread—it doesn't hold up.

1 Preheat the oven to 400°F. Line a 9-inch springform pan with a large sheet of parchment paper, pressing it into the bottom and up the sides of the pan and letting the excess hang over the edge. Place another large piece of parchment in the pan, overlapping the first sheet, and press it in to make sure the entire pan is lined. Don't worry about the creases in the paper—they'll give the cheesecake a beautiful rustic exterior.

2 Using a stand mixer fitted with the paddle attachment, beat the cream cheese, sugar, vanilla, and salt on medium-low speed until very smooth and creamy.

3 Beat in the eggs one at a time so they blend perfectly with the cream cheese.

4 With the mixer running on low, slowly pour in the cream. Add the flour and beat on low to combine.

5 Remove the bowl from the stand mixer and tap it on your counter a few times to push out any air bubbles.

6 Pour the cheesecake into the prepared pan and gently tap it on the counter again.

7 Bake for 45 minutes or until the cheesecake is puffy and the top has darkened to an almost chocolate color. Remove the cheesecake from the oven and let it cool to room temperature, then transfer the entire pan to the fridge, uncovered, to chill for at least 3 hours.

8 When ready to serve, slowly unlock the pan, peel the parchment away from the cheesecake, and cut into slices.

CHEESE SPOTLIGHT: CHAOURCE

#4 in Afrim's Top 13 Hidden-Gem Cheeses (p. 29)

Cheese & Cocktail Pairings

Why does wine get all the fanfare when it comes to cheese pairings? Cocktails are just as deserving, and it's time they got their due. Without further ado, some drinks and cheeses.

The Goat

PREP TIME: 2 MINUTES **SERVES:** 1

Ice

2 oz sparkling wine

1½ oz pomegranate juice

1 oz gin

Fresh pomegranate seeds, for garnish

Grated lime zest, for garnish

3½ oz (100 g) young, fresh goat cheese (the kind you find in a tube in the supermarket)

Your favorite crackers

Growing up in Turkey, my dad developed a deep love for anything pomegranate-related and goat cheese. You might not envision those two flavors together, but here we are. This recipe is for Dad—my boss, my mentor, and the best father ever. An adult version of his favorite childhood snack.

1 To a nice coupe or elegant rocks glass, add a few cubes of ice.

2 Pour in (in this order) the sparkling wine, pomegranate juice, and gin. Stir gently.

3 Garnish with fresh pomegranate seeds and a zesting of lime, and serve with the goat cheese and your favorite crackers.

UNITED KINGDOM

Cucumber Basil Vodka Martini with 2-Year Aged English Cheddar

PREP TIME: 10 MINUTES **SERVES:** 1

4 leaves fresh basil, plus more for garnish

2 oz vodka

1 oz fresh cucumber juice (see note)

½ oz fresh lime juice

½ oz simple syrup (see note)

Ice

Cucumber slice and fresh basil leaf, for garnish

3½ oz (100 g) 2-year aged English cheddar

Compared to North American cheddars, English cheddars are made in a slightly different and more complex way. In England, cheddars are made in drum-like wheels and are clothbound, meaning that the wheels are wrapped in cheesecloth before they are put away to age. In North America, we typically vacuum-pack our cheddars. I think there's room for both styles, but when it comes to drinking a James Bond–inspired martini, you've got to go with England's finest.

1 Place a martini glass in the freezer to chill.

2 In a cocktail shaker, muddle the fresh basil leaves to release their flavor.

3 Add the vodka, cucumber juice, lime juice, and simple syrup to the shaker. Fill with ice, cover, and shake until the drink is chilled.

4 Strain the cocktail into the chilled glass and garnish with a slice of cucumber and fresh basil leaves. Enjoy with the cheddar.

NOTE: To make fresh cucumber juice, grate an English cucumber into a bowl, then strain the juice through a fine-mesh strainer. You can also use a juicer if you have one.

To make simple syrup, heat equal parts granulated sugar and water in a medium saucepan set over medium heat. Once the sugar has dissolved completely, remove the pan from the heat, let the syrup cool, then transfer it to a clean container. The syrup will keep for up to 1 month in the fridge.

The Mighty Negroni with Italian Asiago

PREP TIME: 3 MINUTES **SERVES:** 1

Ice

1 oz gin

1 oz Campari

1 oz sweet vermouth

Orange peel, for garnish

1 splash soda water

3½ oz (100 g) Italian asiago

During the summer of 2023, the only thing I wanted to drink was a classic Negroni. Its bittersweet flavor profile is still my favorite, and pairing it with Italian asiago is the ideal showcase for my Italian heritage. Traditional asiago is made in Veneto, in northern Italy, and it's starkly different from its North American counterpart. Italian asiago is an eating cheese as opposed to a cooking cheese. It has a perfect salty bite that complements the sweetness and bitterness of the Negroni.

1 Chill a rocks glass in the freezer.

2 Fill a mixing glass or shaker with ice. Add the gin, Campari, and sweet vermouth and stir the mixture well for 15–20 seconds to chill and dilute the cocktail slightly.

3 Strain the cocktail into the chilled glass filled with fresh ice.

4 Express the oils from the peel over the cocktail and then twist the peel to release more aroma. Drop the peel into the drink, add a touch of soda water, and enjoy with the asiago.

French 75 with Comté

PREP TIME: 3 MINUTES **SERVES:** 1

Ice

1½ oz gin

¾ oz fresh lemon juice

½ oz simple syrup (see note, p. 154)

Chilled champagne

Cluster of small seedless red grapes, for garnish

3½ oz (100 g) 2-year aged French Comté

My beautiful wife, Courtney, introduced this cocktail to me years ago because she loves champagne and she wanted to get me on board. To be perfectly honest, champagne isn't a drink that I crave, but it works perfectly in this cocktail and paired with French Comté (which also happens to be Courtney's favorite French cheese). I like using a 2-year aged Comté for this—it's rich, nutty, and smooth and works very nicely with the acidity and crispness of the cocktail to make a refreshing summertime snack.

1 Place a champagne flute or coupe in the freezer to chill.

2 Fill a shaker with ice. Add the gin, lemon juice, and simple syrup and shake well until chilled.

3 Strain the drink into the chilled flute or coupe, top with the champagne, and garnish with a cluster of red grapes. Enjoy with the Comté.

NOTE: You can strain the cocktail directly into a highball glass filled with ice and then top it with champagne for a longer and more refreshing drink.

Spanish Fizz with 6-Month Aged Manchego

PREP TIME: 3 MINUTES **SERVES:** 1

Ice

2 oz gin

½ oz elderflower liqueur

¾ oz fresh lime juice

½ oz simple syrup (see note, p. 154)

1 splash soda water

Lime twist or wheels, for garnish

3½ oz (100 g) 6-month aged Spanish manchego

Manchego cheese is the pride of Spain, and it's eaten in many other parts of the world too. It comes in many varying stages of aging, but I prefer the 6-month version with this cocktail, as it has the right amount of tang and salt.

1 Place a highball or Collins glass in the freezer to chill.

2 Fill a shaker with ice. Add the gin, elderflower liqueur, lime juice, and simple syrup. Shake well until chilled.

3 Strain the drink into the chilled glass over fresh ice.

4 Top off the cocktail with club soda to add fizz and effervescence, and give it a gentle stir to mix the ingredients. Garnish with a lime twist or wheels, and enjoy with the manchego.

ARRIVAL
NETHERLANDS

Dutch Mule with 2-Year Aged Beemster

PREP TIME: 3 MINUTES **SERVES:** 1

Ice

2 oz Dutch vodka

½ oz fresh lime juice

½ oz simple syrup (see note, p. 154)

A few splashes ginger beer

Lime wheels or wedge, for garnish

Fresh mint sprig, for garnish

3½ oz (100 g) 2-year aged beemster

This cocktail has a chilled spice to it, so you need a big, bold, intense cheese to pair it with. Beemster comes in various stages of aging. I prefer an older, 2-year version here—it's almost like a salted butterscotch, with a nutty, sharp flavor. Better than candy, if you ask me.

1 Fill a copper mug or highball glass with ice.

2 Fill a shaker with ice. Add the vodka, lime juice, and simple syrup and shake well until chilled.

3 Strain the mixture into the mug or glass.

4 Top off the cocktail with ginger beer to add a refreshing and effervescent element, and give it a gentle stir to mix the ingredients. Garnish with lime wheels or a wedge and a fresh mint sprig, and enjoy with the beemster.

Beerita with Queso Fresco

PREP TIME: 3 MINUTES **SERVES:** 1

½ lime

Kosher salt and lime wedge, for rim

Ice

1½ oz tequila

1 oz triple sec

1 oz fresh lime juice

1 bottle light beer (I love Corona or Modelo for this recipe)

Lime wedge or wheel, for garnish

3½ oz (100 g) queso fresco

Imagine if a beer and a margarita had offspring. This cocktail recipe is just that—the flavor of a classic margarita with the refreshing carbonation of a beer. It's the best of both, ideal for a hot summer day, and will instantly transport you to a gorgeous Mexican beach. This drink calls for a snack of queso fresco, a versatile, lightly flavored, salty cheese that's famous across Latin America.

1 Grate a pinch of lime zest into a bit of salt on a plate. Moisten the rim of a pint glass with a lime wedge and dip it into your lime zest mixture. Fill the pint glass with ice and set aside.

2 Fill a shaker with ice. Add the tequila, triple sec, and lime juice and shake well until chilled.

3 Strain the mixture into the pint glass, top with the beer, and give it a gentle stir to mix the ingredients. Garnish with a lime wedge or wheel, and enjoy with the queso fresco.

A Canadian Cheesy Caesar

PREP TIME: 6 MINUTES **SERVES:** 1

- 3 cherry tomatoes, halved
- 3 balls cherry-sized fresh mozzarella (cherry bocconcini), cut into 9 pieces in total
- Celery salt
- Lime wedge, for rim
- Ice
- 1½ oz vodka
- 4 oz Clamato
- ½ oz fresh lime juice
- 2 dashes hot sauce (Tabasco works great)
- 2 dashes Worcestershire sauce
- 1 pinch freshly ground black pepper
- 3–4 leaves fresh basil, finely chopped, plus a sprig for garnish
- Lime wheels, for garnish
- 3 thin slices Italian prosciutto

With a section of this book dedicated to cocktail and cheese pairings, and as a proud Canadian, how could I not include a Caesar recipe? My version has a cheesy twist, of course. The ingredients in a classic Caesar pair beautifully with fresh mozzarella, and mozzarella, tomatoes, and basil are the holy trinity of flavors that make up a Caprese salad. So I've brought this all together for a great combination that screams "Canada!"

1 First make 3 skewers. Thread the tomato halves and bocconcini pieces in alternating order on each of 3 toothpicks or small skewers. Set aside.

2 Put some celery salt onto a small plate. Moisten the rim of a highball glass with a lime wedge, then dip it into the celery salt. Fill the glass with ice cubes.

3 Pour the vodka over the ice, then add the Clamato, lime juice, hot sauce, Worcestershire, a pinch of celery salt, black pepper, and chopped basil. Stir well to combine all the ingredients. Garnish with a basil sprig.

4 Enjoy by dipping the skewers into your cocktail, with the prosciutto on the side. The cocktail seasons the tomatoes and mozzarella! Cheers.

Uncle Sal's Bourbon Smash with Midnight Moon

PREP TIME: 3 MINUTES **SERVES:** 1

4 leaves fresh mint

2 oz bourbon

½ oz maple syrup

½ oz fresh lemon juice

Crushed ice

Lemon peel, for garnish

Fresh mint sprig, for garnish

3½ oz (100 g) Midnight Moon

One of my dearest friends in the world is Cory Vitiello, who also happens to be one of Toronto's greatest chefs. Years ago, he introduced me to his Uncle Sal, who was looking for some catering for a special family occasion. I brought a ton of tasty food for the party, but as soon as I stepped through the door, Uncle Sal presented me with a cocktail—he's the ultimate host. This drink was phenomenal, and I've been making it ever since. It calls for a big, intensely flavored cheese, so Midnight Moon—a goat cheese made in the Netherlands in collaboration with the iconic Cypress Grove dairy from California—is spot on here. It's made in the classic Dutch gouda style and aged about 1 year to develop those tasty protein crystals and a bold, rich goat flavor. It's one of those IYKYK cheeses.

1 In a shaker, muddle the mint leaves to release their flavor. Add the bourbon, maple syrup, and lemon juice to the shaker, then fill with crushed ice. Shake until well chilled.

2 Strain the mixture into a rocks glass filled with fresh crushed ice, and garnish with a piece of lemon peel and mint sprig. Enjoy with the Midnight Moon.

CHEESE SPOTLIGHT: MIDNIGHT MOON

#8 in Afrim's Top 13 Hidden-Gem Cheeses (p. 30)

Cheese Boards

THE PERFECT CHEESE BOARD

Creating a cheese board should feel like traveling the world. Sometimes you want to visit different countries and regions to showcase different styles and textures of cheese—after all, certain countries and culinary cultures have perfected specific types—so one great way to build a cheese board is to play all the hits. Other times you may want to set up shop in a small town and do a deep dive into that area's strengths. In those situations, it's fun to play the B-sides. Regardless of whether you want a more varied type of cheese board or one that's super specific, the recipes in this chapter are sure to inspire you. But if you want to write your own song, here are some of my top tips for constructing a cheese board of your own.

THE BOARD

Invest in a beautiful live-edge wood board. These are readily available at boutique cheese shops, butcher shops, gift stores, and online. I love a black walnut live-edge board with a fun shape, but you can also go with a classic square or round board. Spending a bit more money on a well-made board will make the cheese pop in presentation, show your guests that you care, and show the cheese the respect it deserves. Plus, if you take care of it properly—wiping the board down with soap and water and brushing it with mineral oil—a good-quality board will last for many, many years.

Now, let's turn to the plating. Overall, you'll want to spread the cheeses out somewhat, giving space between each. Some cheeses can look similar even though their tastes couldn't be more different.

THE CHEESES

When you're constructing your cheese board, play up the contrasts and variety. Keep flavor, aroma, and texture in mind, and make sure that the cheeses and garnishes all work together in perfect harmony. Here is a loose list of suggestions to help you get started. While making your cheese board your own, aim for a similar balance of cow's milk cheese, goat's or sheep's milk cheese, and a wild card like blue cheese.

1 A soft, creamy cow's milk cheese, such as brie
2 A soft goat's or sheep's milk cheese, such as manchego
3 A semisoft cow's milk cheese, such as provolone
4 A firm or aged cow's milk cheese, such as cheddar
5 A blue cheese made from any milk, such as stilton

Wasting great cheese is a sin.

Once you've selected your cheeses, you have to determine the number of people you're feeding. You don't want to under-buy, but you don't want to overdo it either—wasting great cheese is a sin. If you're working with five different styles of cheese, I suggest buying 1–1½ oz (30–45 g) of each cheese per person. For example, if you're planning to serve four people, you'd buy five types of cheese that each weigh 4–6 oz (115–170 g).

PLATING

For the suggested types of cheese, try arranging them as follows:
1 Leave the soft, creamy cow's milk cheese in the shape you bought it in. Don't cut up a gorgeous wheel of brie; let the guests see what it looks like in its original state, and let guests serve themselves with a small cheese knife.

2 Ditto for the soft goat's or sheep's milk cheese—let it be.

3 Cut the semisoft cow's milk cheese into small triangular slices. Here is where you can get creative on a board. Sometimes I'll create an almost X shape with the triangular pieces, and other times I'll line them up simply from north to south on the board. Play around with it.

4 Chunk up the firm or aged cow's milk cheese in a rustic way. You can gently chip away at the block so the cheese almost crumbles, but keep it chunky. Doing it this way showcases that these cheeses are made by hand. Often people cut firm cheese into perfect cubes, but I don't love this approach. Cheese isn't perfect. These are handmade products that can have slight imperfections, and that's the honest and noble part about cheese making that speaks to me. Once you've got your rustic cheese pieces, pile them up together nicely.

5 Serve the blue cheese as a wedge. Its uniquely creamy and crumbly texture looks best that way, so don't slice or chunk it. Let the blue veins shine and be prominent.

ACCOMPANIMENTS

Now we need a few other ingredients to make the ultimate cheese board. Like the contrasting cheeses you've selected, you want contrasting flavors and textures for your garnishes.

First up is a fresh, crusty baguette. It's classic for a reason. The neutral flavor is perfect for creamier cheeses.

Another fun vessel is a fruit and nut crisp, like walnut-raisin or apricot-pistachio crisps. These pair beautifully with firmer, more robust, saltier cheeses and blue cheese. Between these two bread products, you'll have your bases covered.

Water-based fruits are a must—think fresh apples, pears, grapes, and figs. Their high water content and acidity levels make them wonderful palate cleansers as you travel through the various cheeses on your board.

You'll also want something sweet. Try a fig jam, a strawberry jam, or a dried fruit like apricots or dried cherries. Placing the jam in a ramekin is a nice touch, but either way, the color of the jam and fruit will brighten up the board. And you'll need a savory component as well. Try red pepper jelly, caramelized onion jam, aged balsamic vinegar, or a savory chutney. There are hundreds of options, so pick what you like or try something new from your local cheese shop.

I also like to include one or two cured meats, like a sliced prosciutto, serrano ham, milk salami, or sausage. If you're including meat, don't choose anything spicy, as it could overshadow the nuances of the cheeses.

DRINKS RECOMMENDATIONS

Lastly, you'll need something to quench your thirst. You can go the cocktail route (see pp. 151–169), or stick with wine. For white, I like a chilled Riesling, which has a freshness and acidity that complements the creamy or more funky cheeses. For red, I like Cabernet Franc, which is typically medium-bodied with ripe fruit on the palate, and again, great acidity. Because cheese is fat, the acidity in the wine is important to help cut through the richness.

The most important thing to remember is that none of these suggestions are set in stone. I'm here to be your tour guide, but at some point, you need to choose your own adventure. Have fun with it, experiment, and keep track of what works and what doesn't. That's the best part!

All-French Cheese Board

PREP TIME: 10 MINUTES **SERVES:** 6

France produces some of the best and most iconic cheeses I've ever had. And one of the strengths in French cheese making is the amazing diversity in the products. In their varying styles, textures, and flavor profiles, the French do it all and they do it very well. In this cheese board, I've showcased the beautiful landscape of French cheese along with some classic accompaniments. Make sure to enjoy this board with some great French wine. See pp. 172–174 for instructions on how to build your board.

CHEESES:

5 oz (140 g) Comté (French Alps)

5 oz (140 g) Brie de Meaux (Île-de-France)

5 oz (140 g) Chabichou (Loire Valley)

5 oz (140 g) Papillon Noir Roquefort (Aveyron)

5 oz (140 g) Morbier (French Alps)

5 oz (140 g) Ossau-Iraty (Pyrenees)

5 oz (140 g) aged Mimolette (Normandy)

ACCOMPANIMENTS:

French prunes

French picholine or Nicoise olives

Walnuts

Your favorite sweet French jam or jelly

Seedless green grapes

Good-quality dry-cured French sausage, sliced

Crusty baguette

DRINK RECOMMENDATIONS:

French Chenin Blanc

Burgundy Pinot Noir

Banyuls

Spanish Manchego Tasting

PREP TIME: 10 MINUTES **SERVES:** 4–6

Manchego is one of the most popular cheeses in Spain and possibly in the world. It's a crucial ingredient in so many classic Spanish dishes, but I thought it would be fun to break it down and do a deep dive. It's amazing what you can taste when you examine the difference that aging or flavor infusions make. The garnishes on this board are some of the best food products that Spain has to offer, and they're a lovely way to immerse yourself in the culture. See pp. 172–174 for instructions on how to build your board.

CHEESES:

5 oz (140 g) 3-month aged manchego

5 oz (140 g) 6-month aged manchego

5 oz (140 g) 1-year aged manchego

5 oz (140 g) manchego rubbed in olive oil

5 oz (140 g) black truffle–infused manchego

ACCOMPANIMENTS:

5 oz (140 g) chorizo sausage

Marcona almonds

1 small jar pickled red Spanish peppers

Membrillo (an authentic Spanish quince paste)

Tortas (sweet and savory biscuits)

Seedless green grapes

DRINK RECOMMENDATIONS:

Cava

Sherry

Tempranillo

Quebec Cheese Board

PREP TIME: 10 MINUTES **SERVES:** 4–6

Quebec has had a strong cheese culture for over a century. Cheese-making recipes for Oka, cheese curds, cheddar, and so much more have long been an integral part of Quebec food culture, and new and exciting products are always being introduced to Canadians across the country too. After seeing a huge cheese boom in Quebec in the early 2000s, I was interested to see where it would go. Twenty-five years later, Quebec is producing some of the world's best dairy products, and believe me, it goes well beyond Oka and cheese curds. See pp. 172–174 for instructions on how to build your board.

CHEESES:

5 oz (140 g) Grey Owl goat cheese

5 oz (140 g) Riopelle

5 oz (140 g) Le Douanier

5 oz (140 g) Louis D'or

5 oz (140 g) Ermite blue

ACCOMPANIMENTS:

Honeycrisp apple

Quebec honey

Your favorite crackers

Ice wine jelly

Pecans

DRINK RECOMMENDATIONS:

Quebec-produced hard cider

Ice wine

Cabernet Franc

ITALY

DEPARTED

Spritz O'Clock & Snacks

PREP TIME: 10 MINUTES **SERVES:** 4

CHEESES:

5 oz (140 g) Piave cheese (preferably 1-year aged)

5 oz (140 g) Friulano cheese

ACCOMPANIMENTS:

5 oz (140 g) soppressata, thinly sliced

5 oz (140 g) olive oil–marinated artichoke hearts

Good-quality salt-flavored kettle chips

Green Bella di Cerignola olives

Italian fennel taralli

Good-quality orange jam or marmalade

Spiced mixed nuts

Baguette, sliced and toasted

APEROL SPRITZ:

Ice

2½ oz prosecco

1½ oz Aperol

¾ oz club soda

1 medium-thick orange slice

Is there anything better in the world than a beautiful summer day paired with an ice-cold Aperol spritz, cheese, and a few other snacks? No, there isn't. This is the ultimate combination. The Aperol spritz cocktail has taken the world by storm over the last 10 years. What started off as a classic northern Italian beverage is now possibly the most popular cocktail on the planet, and with good reason. It's refreshing, easy to make, and unique. What's not to love? Here's a board celebrating this drink and the cheeses that work best with it. See pp. 172–174 for instructions on how to build your board.

1 To make the Aperol spritz, fill a large stemmed red wine glass three-quarters of the way with ice. Add the prosecco, Aperol, and club soda and gently stir to combine. Drop in the orange slice or place it on the edge of the glass as a garnish.

Prosciutto Lovers with a Side of Cheese

PREP TIME: 10 MINUTES **SERVES:** 4 HUNGRY PROSCIUTTO FANS

Prosciutto is a beautiful thing—a salted pork leg that has been air-cured for many months or even years. Italy obviously gets a lot of the fanfare when it comes to prosciutto, but this board showcases the wide and wonderful world of this cured meat. It's a great example of terroir and how different countries treat their cured pork legs. Here I'm highlighting Italy, Spain, and France. I wasn't going to add any cheese to this board, but then what kind of a cheese board would this be? So I chose a fun, classic cheese from each country as well as a wine. Which will reign supreme? You tell me. See pp. 172–174 for instructions on how to build your board.

PROSCIUTTO:

16 slices prosciutto di Parma (Italy)

16 slices jambon de Bayonne (France)

16 slices serrano ham (Spain)

CHEESES:

5 oz (140 g) Parmigiano-Reggiano (Italy)

5 oz (140 g) Comté (France)

5 oz (140 g) manchego (Spain)

ACCOMPANIMENTS:

Grissini breadsticks

Cantaloupe

Black olives

Seedless red grapes

Bartlett pear

Fresh figs

Gooseberries

DRINK RECOMMENDATIONS:

Nebbiolo (Italy)

Pinot Noir (France)

Rioja (Spain)

A Cheesy Butter Board

PREP TIME: 15 MINUTES **SERVES:** 3–4

1 cup salted butter, room temperature

¼ cup chopped Marcona almonds

2 Tbsp chili-infused honey

3½ oz (100 g) Parmigiano-Reggiano, finely grated

2 sprigs fresh thyme, leaves picked

Zest of 1 medium orange

Edible flowers, for garnish

1 baguette, sliced and toasted

DRINK RECOMMENDATIONS:

Champagne

Chenin Blanc

The year was 2022 and the "butter board" had taken social media by storm. It was everywhere. Listen, am I a few years late to this trend? Yes. But butter and bread might be the best food combination ever, and I couldn't resist adding my own cheesy spin on it. It's simple, but it works. Buy the very best butter you can afford here—local, organic, grass-fed butter will make a big difference to the result.

1 Smear the butter all over a cheese board to cover most of the surface, but leave a 1-inch border on each side.

2 Scatter the almonds overtop, then drizzle with the honey and sprinkle with the grated Parmigiano-Reggiano. Sprinkle with the thyme leaves and orange zest, and garnish with the edible flowers. Enjoy spread onto pieces of toasted baguette.

Ontario Cheese Board

PREP TIME: 10 MINUTES **SERVES:** 4–6

I'm proud to be from Toronto, Ontario, for many reasons, and over the last decade or so, I can add cheese to that list. For decades, we were known for fresh cheese curds and aged cheddars, but in the last 10 years, the Ontario dairy industry has turned its focus to other styles of cheese, and the results have been fantastic. It's an exciting time for us and our cheese industry right now, and the sky's the limit. Look out world, we are coming for you. This board features Ontario's greatest hits. See pp. 172–174 for instructions on how to build your board.

CHEESES:

5 oz (140 g) 5-year aged Ontario cheddar

5 oz (140 g) 3-year aged Mountainoak gouda

5 oz (140 g) Bel Haven Triple Crème Brie

5 oz (140 g) 5 Brothers

5 oz (140 g) Wildwood

5 oz (140 g) Celtic Blue

ACCOMPANIMENTS:

Ontario honeycomb

Red pepper jelly

Your favorite crackers

Peanuts (Ontario grows amazing peanuts—who knew?)

Good-quality pepperoni-style sausage, thinly sliced

DRINK RECOMMENDATIONS:

Cabernet Franc from the Niagara region

Chardonnay from the Niagara region (try to find an oak-forward one)

Ontario craft IPA beer

After-Dinner English Cheese Board

PREP TIME: 10 MINUTES **SERVES:** 4–6

I can't be absolutely sure, but I'd hazard a guess that the English were one of the first countries to indulge in the after-dinner cheese board. Nothing goes better with leftover red wine after dinner, but a glass of vintage port is lovely as well. Here is a traditional English-inspired cheese board with all the fixings. You'll note that English cheeses tend to lean more toward the firm/aged side, so you won't see a brie or softer style of cheese here. See pp. 172–174 for instructions on how to build your board.

CHEESES:

5 oz (140 g) English stilton

5 oz (140 g) Red Leicester

5 oz (140 g) smoked applewood cheddar

5 oz (140 g) 2-year aged traditional English cheddar

5 oz (140 g) mango ginger stilton

ACCOMPANIMENTS:

Medjool dates

Caramelized onion jam

Chili jam

Oatcakes (a classic biscuit for English cheese)

Bartlett pear

Good-quality shortbread (I know it's Scottish, but it works well with stilton)

DRINK RECOMMENDATIONS:

Whatever red wine you have left over from dinner

Vintage port (I love a 10-year tawny port)

Scotch (I love a 10- or 20-year single malt scotch)

The Ultimate Italian Cheese Board

PREP TIME: 10 MINUTES **SERVES:** 4–6

Italy is responsible for some of the most amazing and iconic cheeses ever made. You can find so many different styles, textures, and flavor profiles, from bufala mozzarella in southern Italy to Parmigiano-Reggiano in northern Italy, and many beauties in between. Cheese is an enormous part of Italian culture and cuisine, and this board represents the best from all over the country. It's perfect for a long Sunday lunch. See pp. 172–174 for instructions on how to build your board.

CHEESES:

5 oz (140 g) 5-year aged Parmigiano-Reggiano (Emilia-Romagna)

5 oz (140 g) Taleggio (Lombardy)

5 oz (140 g) Brillo (Tuscany)

5 oz (140 g) Moliterno (Sardinia)

5 oz (140 g) La Tur (Piedmont)

5 oz (140 g) Gorgonzola (Lombardy)

ACCOMPANIMENTS:

Abate Italian pear or Anjou pear

Mostarda (a condiment of caramelized fruits in a mustard-seed syrup)

Panettone (if you're making this board when Panettone is available, typically November to January, it pairs wonderfully with the La Tur and Gorgonzola)

Italian torrone nougat

6- or 10-year aged balsamic vinegar

Flatbread

Mixed olives

DRINK RECOMMENDATIONS:

Amaro

Vin Santo

Nebbiolo

ARRIVAL
NETHERLANDS

All-Dutch Cheese Board

PREP TIME: 10 MINUTES **SERVES:** 4–6

The Netherlands makes incredible cheese, there's no question about that. However, the styles of cheese made there are quite similar to each other. The Dutch don't produce brie-style cheeses, blue cheeses, or sheep cheeses. But in the same way that a deep dive into Spanish manchego (p. 22) can teach us about Spanish culinary culture, the choices showcased in this Dutch-centered board are a fantastic demonstration of what the aging process can do for firm cheeses. I adore this board, and I hope you will too. See pp. 172–174 for instructions on how to build your board.

CHEESES:

5 oz (140 g) 1-year aged Dutch gouda

5 oz (140 g) 3-year aged (or older) Dutch gouda

5 oz (140 g) 1-year aged beemster

5 oz (140 g) 3-year aged beemster

5 oz (140 g) Prima Donna maturo

5 oz (140 g) Prima Donna forte

5 oz (140 g) Dutch goat gouda

ACCOMPANIMENTS:

Apricot jam

Apple jelly

Fruit and nut crisps

Crusty baguette

Good-quality butter (the move is to smother butter on your baguette and top with a slice of cheese)

Chili-infused honey

Seedless green or red grapes

12 thin slices Italian prosciutto (I know, it's not very Dutch, but it works with these cheeses!)

DRINK RECOMMENDATIONS:

Off-dry Reisling

Merlot

Prosecco

Old Amsterdam

Old Amsterdam

Afrim Pristine
CHEESE BOUTIQUE
IGOR
Gorgonzola
DOLCE
Donna
ASIAGO

ACKNOWLEDGMENTS

Growing up in the west end of Toronto, I never thought I would have published one book, let alone two. I am so blessed to have this this opportunity—thank you to the team at Penguin Random House Canada, and Appetite in particular. I will never forget the conversation I had with the publisher of Appetite, Robert McCullough, about this second book. I was traveling in Crete, filming my TV series, *Cheese: A Love Story*, when Robert called and asked what I thought about writing a second book. In all honesty, seeing how much work I had to put into the first book, I'd said to myself that I was done—I left all my ink on the paper. But after chatting with Robert, we both decided that a second book was a great idea. I realized that I wasn't done telling my story. That day, I also told Robert that I wouldn't want to do this with any editor besides Zoe Maslow, who edited my first book. Zoe is my friend, she is the best at what she does, and she's become my true confidant. When the going got tough and I got behind on my deadlines, Zoe was there to coach me through it all. I love you Zoe, like a sister.

To my parents, Fatos and Modesta Pristine. You have helped shape me as a good human being, guide me through life, and sacrifice so much for my brothers and me. Now that I'm a parent, I respect you even more. You started Cheese Boutique, and I'm just trying to keep your legacy going—this book adds to your story, as well as mine.

To my brother Agim. You're my business partner, my eldest brother, and my role model for the last 45 years. You are the vision behind Cheese Boutique, and you don't get enough credit for everything that you do. If Cheese Boutique is a car, you're the engine. We don't say, "I love you" very often, but I know we feel it by how well we work together.

To my sister-in-law Sophia. Before I met my wife, Courtney, Sophia was my emergency contact and I still trust her with my life. Whenever I travel, she is the first person I text to say I've landed safely. She's been in our family for 35 years and I can't imagine a better sister.

To my brother Ilir. You are one of the most talented and creative people I've ever met. You're invaluable to Cheese Boutique, and I have always been inspired by your free spirit.

To my younger brother, Arian, who passed away June 8, 2020. You were the best of all the boys in our family. You didn't need the limelight, you helped raise two amazing kids with my incredibly loyal sister-in-law Melissa. I miss you and love you, Krods.

To all my family all over the world. My aunts, uncles, cousins, nieces, and nephews. There are bits and pieces of you throughout this book. I love you all.

To my in-laws, the Bull family, or my Niagara family, as I've called you for so many years. Mama Bull, Papa Bull, LB, Zachary, Nimbot, Livi, Benjamin, Mila, and Frankie. Thank you for immediately welcoming me into your amazing family. My crazy fits your crazy like a glove.

To the great chefs, sommeliers, and culinary folks who I've learned from and been inspired by. Each chef who has stepped into Cheese Boutique has shaped me in one way or another. I like to think I'm a bit of a sponge—I love to learn, and I'm always on the hunt for new and interesting ways to cook. Thank you for all that you've taught me.

To the entire Cheese Boutique staff. We've been open for 55 years! Such longevity is so rare these days. I've been so lucky to work alongside people I love and respect, and I thank you for putting your hearts and souls into my family business.

Blessed are the cheese makers. I can't do my job without your blood, sweat, and tears. The life of a cheese maker is about pure passion. They don't do it to become millionaires or to see their name in the lights. They do it because they love it. Taking milk and salt and creating something so stinky, so sharp, so aged, so goaty, and so on is truly an art form. This book doesn't happen without your works of art. To be a cheese maker is to be an alchemist: you turn milk into gold.

Lastly, to my wife, Courtney, and my son, Leonardo. You two are the most important people in my life.

Courtney, you are the absolute best support system and my best friend, and I couldn't imagine doing any of this without you. You are my rock when I get home from a long day. You understand when I need time to rest, and you know when to push me to be the best I can be. Where I am the realist in our lives, you are the absolute dreamer. You reach for the stars with our family, you dream up a life we both want, and we are slowly getting there. I love you with every fiber of my being. You also happen to be an incredible cook, and I've learned so much from you in the kitchen.

To my sweet boy, Leonardo, you are a miracle in more ways than one. Your smile and love can turn my mood around instantly. When you say "Daddy," I melt like a 90-day aged brie in the hot sun. This book is ultimately for you. This book is for you to brag to your friends one day. This book is for you to show your kids one day. This book is for you to realize that without cheese, our family has nothing. Love it like I do, my sweet boy. You mean everything to me, and I can't wait to enjoy cheese with you the way my dad did with me.

INDEX

NOTE: Page numbers in bold type indicate photographs.

GERMANY
GREECE
WELCOME TO MEXICO
ARRIVAL
INDIA
USA
ARRIVAL
SOUTH KOREA
LONDON
ENGLAND
WELCOME TO NEW DELHI
INDIA
CONTROL
NORWAY
COPENHAGEN
DENMARK
DEPARTED
WELCOME TO
CANADA
BIENVENUE AU
ZURICH AIRPORT
SWITZERLAND
ARRIVAL
SWISS CONFEDERATION
A.B.C
GREECE
ATHENS
CYPRUS
LARNACA INTERNATIONAL AIRPORT
THAILAND
ARRIVAL
GERMANY
TURKEY
ANKARA INTERNATIONAL AIRPORT
WELCOME
FRANCE
ARRIVAL
ARGENTINA
SPAIN